Lothian

Lothian

A Historical Guide

Mark Collard

Birlinn

For Helen, without whom...

First published in Great Britain, 1998,
Birlinn Limited
Canongate Venture
5 New Street
Edinburgh EH8 8BH
info@birlinn.co.uk

British Library Cataloguing-in-Publication Date
A Catalogue record for this book is available from the British Library.

ISBN 1 874744 45 9

Cover picture acknowledgements: Clockwise from the top:

Pilgrim Token Mould, North Berwick
Apprentice Pillar, Roslin Chapel © George Petrie/Royal Commission
        on the Ancient and Historical Monuments of Scotland
The Bass Rock from *Voyage Round Great Britain* by William Daniell, by
        courtesy of the Mitchell Library, Glasgow City Libraries and Archives
Temple, Old Churchyard, Midlothian © Mark Collard

Typeset in Plantin by Mitchell Graphics, Glasgow

Printed and bound in Finland by Werner Söderström OY

CONTENTS

Site Plans, Maps and Plates   vii

Introduction   1

The Palaeolithic Period: *c.*500,000 – 7000 BC   4

Mesolithic Hunter-Gatherers: *c.*7000 – 3500 BC   6

The Neolithic Period: *c.*4000 – 2500 BC   8

The Early and Middle Bronze Age: *c.*2500 – 1000 BC   12
    Late Neolithic Bronze Age Sites   17
        Standing Stones   17
        Stone Circles   18
        Cairns   19
        Cup-and-ring marks   22

The Late Bronze Age and Pre-Roman Iron Age:
  1000 BC – 43 AD   23
    Iron Age Sites   28
        Palisaded enclosures   28
        Forts   31
        Unenclosed settlements   38
        Scooped settlements   38

The Roman Iron Age: 43 – 410 AD   40
    Roman Sites   45
        Forts   45
        Temporary camps   47
        Roads   48
    Souterrains   49

Early Historic Period: 400 – 1100 AD   51
    Dark Age Sites   55

Settlements   55
Religious sites   55

The Countryside: 1100 – 1900 AD   58
    Agricultural Sites   62
        Mills   62
        Windmills   65
        Steadings   66
        Teind barn   67

The Towns of Lothian: 1100 – 1600 AD   68
    Burghs   71

Churches and Religious Houses: 1100 – 1900 AD   75
    Medieval religious houses   78
    Parish and collegiate churches   84
    Post-Reformation churches: 1500 – 1900 AD   95
    Post-Reformation gravestones   97

Castles and Large Houses: 1100 – 1900 AD   99
    Castles, tower-houses and laird's houses:
        1100 – 1800 AD   102
    Country houses: 1700 – 1900 AD   127

Industry and Communications: 1600 – 1900 AD   131
    Industrial Sites   135
        Mining   135
        Oil-shale workings   138
        Brickworks   138
        Limekilns   138
        Paper mills   140
        Weaving   140
        Railways   140
        Brewing   141
        Canals   141
        Harbours   142

Bibliography and Further Reading   143

Museums to Visit   144

SITE PLANS

1. St Mary's Whitekirk. Plans of the Tithe Barn (**31**)   67
2. Newbattle Abbey. Plan (**8**)   82
3. St Michael's Parish Church. Plan (**39**)   91
4. Uphall Church. Plan (**52**)   94
5. Pencaitland Church. Plan (**61**)   97
6. Barnes Castle. Plan and view (**5**)   105
7. Crichton Castle. Section through courtyard and keep, looking North (**21**)   110
8. Linlithgow Palace. Plan of ground floor (**48**)   117
9. Tantallon Castle. Plan of site (**72**)   124

MAPS

1. The Neolithic Period   16
2. The Late Bronze Age and Pre-Roman Age   29
3. The Roman Iron Age   46
4. Dark Age Sites   56
5. The Countryside   63
6. Churches and Religious Houses   79
7. Castles   103
8. Country Houses 1700 – 1900   128
9. Industrial Sites   136

PLATES

1   The Loth Stone and Traprain Law

2   Cairnpapple Henge, Cairn and Stone Circle

3   Windmill at Balgone near North Berwick

4   Papple Steading near Whittingehame

5   The village Tron and Old Parish Church Tower at Stenton

6   Temple Preceptory

7   Dunglass Collegiate Chapel

8   Gifford Parish Kirk

9   Seventeenth-century gravestones at Tranent Parish Church

10 Linlithgow Palace

11 Niddry Castle and shale bing, near Winchburgh

12 Borthwick Castle

13 Limekilns at Catcraig near Dunbar

14 Beam pumping engine at Prestongrange

15 Hoffman brick-kiln at Prestongrange

16 Miners' cottages at Rosewell

INTRODUCTION

Bounded to the north by the Firth of Forth, to the west by the Bathgate Hills and to the south and east by the hills of the Southern Uplands, Lothian forms a natural geographic unit. It is cut by four rivers, running north to south, fed from burns rising in the watershed of the surrounding hills. None are of any great size, but all are prone to spate and flood in heavy rain. The land is among the most fertile in Scotland, ranging from heavier clay in West Lothian, most suited to grazing, through to the lighter soils of the east, which produce heavy arable crops. The river valleys provide lighter, productive soils even within the areas of heavy clay. The upland areas provide rough grazing only, although they were not always the often bleak moorland which is typical today. The main mineral resources of Lothian were the large coalfields of all three counties and the oil-bearing shales of West Lothian. Good quality building stone is readily available in most areas. To the north the sea was rich in fish and shellfish.

The name Lothian for the whole area is known from the 16th century, although its antiquity beyond that is uncertain. It was divided into three counties, West, East and Midlothian. In the 19th century these were known by the names of the three county towns, Haddingtonshire, Linlithgowshire and Edinburghshire, but the old names were restored earlier this century. They survive the local govern-ment reorganisation of 1996, with the continuing separation of a fourth administrative area, the City of Edinburgh, created in 1974. Edinburgh has long dominated the history of the whole region, and the sheer quantity of information about its history and buildings led to the decision to publish this volume about the rest of Lothian separately. The boundaries used as limits are those defined in 1974, when areas to the west and south were lost to Central and Borders Region.

Lothian has been an attractive settlement location for more than 6000 years. The evidence for this settlement, however, is very uneven in its preservation. The fragility of many of the earlier prehistoric remains means that they have often survived the centuries badly, as the land of Lothian has been constantly disturbed by agriculture, mineral extraction and industry. Chance finds of artefacts or burials are the only evidence for prehistoric settlement of large areas. Monuments standing above ground-level survive best in the marginal areas of the uplands. In the lower areas, sites have often been ploughed flat, but their existence is known from marks visible from the air in growing crops. Most of these cropmark sites are in East Lothian, where the soils are particularly conducive to the formation of cropmarks. Further west the grasslands and hilly areas do not produce the same results; furthermore the absence of ground disturbance by ploughing means that artefacts from buried remains come to the surface less often. All these factors should be borne in mind when considering the maps of distribution of sites from the earlier periods.

Within this volume, those sites which have visible remains and can be certainly attributed to a reasonably accurate date have been included. There are many sites in Lothian, particularly those known only from aerial photographs, which cannot be securely identified as having a particular date or function, and, to avoid any dubiety, they have been excluded. Furthermore it is an unwritten law of archaeology that sites, when excavated, prove to be far more complicated in their periods of occupation and function than appears to be the case from their surface appearance. This should always be borne in mind as a caveat when considering the sites in this volume.

For ease of narrative and reference, the prehistoric period has been described in this book using the traditional 'three age' system, of Stone Age, Bronze Age and Iron Age, a system devised in the 19th century. It has become increasingly clear that change within prehistoric societies was far more complex than technological 'advances' in toolmaking. Thus it was decided that, to a limited degree, the arrangement of the chapters within this book should reflect this change in thinking.

Many of the sites mentioned in this volume are marked on the Ordnance Survey maps of the area. The best maps are the 1:25,000 scale *Pathfinder Series* which are particularly detailed, although many are required to cover the whole area. Three maps of the smaller-scale *Landranger Series* (nos. 65, 66 and 67) cover the whole of Lothian.

One of the main aims of this book is to encourage visits to the visible remains of Lothian's past. Sites of particular interest or good survival are marked with an asterisk.

It must be stressed, however, that many of the sites lie on private land, and no legal right of access is guaranteed. Permission to visit sites, particularly the residences of the later period, should always be sought. The countryside code should be observed at all times in rural areas. Care should be taken when exploring industrial landscapes, as many old mineworkings are not marked or easily visible, and personal injury is easy. Particular care should also be taken to ensure that sites of any period are not disturbed at all by visits.

Sites marked with an asterisk (*) are in the guardianship of the Secretary of State for Scotland, the National Trust for Scotland, or are opened on a regular basis by their private owners. Most of the asterisk-marked sites are subject to standard Historic Scotland opening times and regulations. It may be worth checking with Historic Scotland in Edinburgh (0131-668-8600) or the Scottish Tourist Board (0131-332-2433) any regulations which may apply to a site you wish to visit.

THE PALAEOLITHIC PERIOD
c.500,000 – 7000 BC

For much of the past half a million years, the land mass of Britain has seen a series of major Ice Ages. Four major episodes of glaciation are known, each lasting tens of thousands of years. Between the advances of the ice-caps were warmer periods, when the ice retreated, either for short periods within the main Ice Ages (known as interstadial periods) or during longer warmer spells (interglacials). Humans are now known to have hunted in Britain since at least 500,000 BC. These early inhabitants, *homo erectus* and later, *homo sapiens neanderthalensis*, were the ancestors of modern human beings (*homo sapiens sapiens*) who arrived around 40,000 BC. They lived in and around the ice-sheets and tundra of the successive Ice Ages, and exploited periods of recession of the ice cover, hunting the abundant wildlife.

It is certain that the area of Scotland would have been habitable for considerable periods during the interglacial and interstadial warming of the climate; the example of modern Inuit peoples show that life is possible even in severe cold conditions. It is unfortunate that the continual scouring of the glaciers and the associated movement of considerable quantities of rock, gravel and sand seem to have eradicated or obscured all traces of these early hunters, and, as yet, there is no certain evidence for their presence in Scotland.

The scouring and gouging of the glaciers created the underlying land form familiar today and which gives Scotland its particular landscape character. Combined with the soils which subsequently developed over the land, and the climate, this has been the basis for all aspects of human activity over the 9000 years since humans returned to settle more permanently, acting as both opportunity and constraint.

The final act of the last Ice Age began about 23,000 BC as the ice moved south, reaching its greatest extent around 18,000 BC, when it covered the whole of Scotland. The retreat began about 15,000 BC, and with the exception of a cold period (11,000–10,000 BC) there was a gradual improvement

4

from cold tundra, through the gradual formation of soils, to the development of woodland cover. With these climate and landscape changes came the development of diverse flora and fauna, and ultimately human beings returned to exploit the rich natural resources.

MESOLITHIC HUNTER-GATHERERS
c.7000 – 3500 BC

The settlers who gradually colonised the new land lived by exploiting the abundant natural resources available, and are referred to as hunter-gatherers. It seems that the earliest settlers moved into Scotland from several different directions, along the west and east coasts from the south and also from the north, although at present the earliest known sites are all on western islands such as Rum (7000 BC), Islay, Jura and Arran (all c.6000 BC). The settlers were nomadic, establishing camps in different locations around their territories, placed according to the season and the available food and resources. It seems that they returned to these sites each year. The distribution of known sites suggests that the coastal strip and river valleys were, not surprisingly, the favoured settlement locations with their abundant natural resources and ease of travel where the woodland cover was thinner. The settlers seemed to have been immensely adaptable and skilled, fishing both from rivers and at sea, using boats made of dug-out logs or skins, hunting and trapping the animals of the woodland and gathering a wide range of foodstuffs including plants, berries and edible shellfish. Pebbles of flint and chert were skilfully flaked to make a wide range of tools for the acquisition of food by hunting and fishing, and also for the processing of these foodstuffs. These flint tools were generally very small and are known as 'microliths' (literally 'small stones'). Other tools were made of bone, including harpoons and mattocks.

The need for mobility meant that their homes were generally portable shelters made by stretching hides over frameworks of branches. Unfortunately these leave little trace archaeologically and consequently sites of this period are very difficult to discover. Very often the only trace of their existence is a scatter of flint or stone tools, or the accumulated debris of their camp-sites, particularly shell middens along the coast. In Lothian it is usually only these flint scatters which give a hint of the presence of the hunter-gatherers, despite the fact that the area must have been an attractive settlement location. Recent excavations at Cramond (Edinburgh), close to the mouth of the River Almond have produced the first evidence of actual settlement, with large quantities of flint debris and tools found in association with a pit containing hazelnut shells and evidence for the holes made by the timber frames of shelters or windbreaks. The other sites in Lothian which have produced flint artefacts reinforce the idea of coastal and valley settlement, with finds of groups of flint tools made at several scattered locations such as Aberlady, North Berwick, Hedderwick and Torness in East Lothian, Inveresk at the mouth of the Esk and, further south along the Esk valley, at Elginhaugh near Dalkeith.

THE NEOLITHIC PERIOD
c.4000 – 2500 BC

The five hundred years before 3500 BC saw a fundamental change in the settlement of Britain, the impact of which continues today. That change was the introduction of agriculture – the use of land for the deliberate cultivation of crops and the rearing of domestic animals. This was not a sudden happening; it has become increasingly clear from archaeological fieldwork that the later groups of hunter-gatherers had become far less mobile, establishing semi-permanent camp-sites and reducing the size of the territories each group exploited; becoming, in effect, almost permanent settlers. Such a framework allowed the new ideas and techniques to spread relatively rapidly through the country.

Farming had spread erratically through western Europe from about 5500 BC. Its introduction to Britain has been seen as the result of invasion or colonisation by technologically more advanced peoples arriving from the Continent, or by the diffusion of ideas and technology from a single point of discovery. The truth is most likely a complex mixture of both, added to local innovation and adaptation. It is certain, however, that the essentials of agriculture, the domesticated animals such as sheep and seed crops, were introduced from abroad as they did not occur naturally in Britain. Interestingly, the earliest farming settlements away from the mainland of Europe occur in Ireland.

Along with the raw materials of farming came new tools and technologies: the polished stone axe essential for clearing woodland; spades and ards for turning the soil; new types of flint tools such as sickles for harvesting wheat and barley crops; quernstones for processing them; pottery for storage were all introductions in this period, supplementing the hunting and fishing tool-kit of the hunter-gatherers.

The most immediate effect of the new technology seems to have been the clearance of the woodland which still covered much of Britain to allow the planting of crops and grazing of animals. Obviously this was not a single event, but a gradual process as the population increased. This clearance began almost simultaneously in many different parts of the country.

While agriculture did become the main source of food, it is clear that the old techniques of hunting and gathering played a fundamental part in the subsistence farming of Britain for many thousands of years, providing not only the necessary raw materials for tools and equipment, but also supplementary food, particularly valuable in times of crop failure.

The regular cultivation of land and keeping of herds of animals saw a further change in the character of settlement with the establishment of permanently settled extended families exploiting defined areas of land; the nomadic lifestyle of the hunter-gatherers was supplanted by the regular demands of the farming calendar. Very few of the earliest farms have survived. Often their presence is shown only by the presence of finds of artefacts such as stone axes. As yet no settlements have been found in Lothian, but the presence of fine polished axes from many parts of Lothian show that the early farmers were active in this area.

The best-preserved and most widely investigated farms of this period are those of the Northern Isles, particularly Orkney. Here the local building material was stone and the houses of these early settlements have survived. At Skara Brae a small village was occupied for more than 600 years from *c.* 3300 BC onwards.

Internally the houses were roughly square, single rooms with central hearths with furniture such as beds, dressers and cupboards arranged around the walls, all built of stone. At Knap of Howar on Papa Westray a different house type was excavated, again built of stone, but rectangular and divided internally into separate rooms by upright slabs. Elsewhere in Scotland, particularly in the south and east, the buildings would have been of timber and their remains often have not survived. However an example of this type of house was excavated at Balbridie in Grampian and shown to be a large rectangular building, 26 metres long and 13 metres wide, with walls of upright timbers.

The commonest and best preserved monuments of this period are the monumental tombs of some of the early farmers

which seem to have been built from around 4000 BC
onwards. Mostly built of stone, usually rectangular, they are
often known as chambered or passage tombs and occur in
many parts of Scotland and it is possible to identify distinct
local types in different regions. Many of those which have
been investigated have shown a long and complex development, sometimes starting as a single chamber before the
addition of further chambers. The common element of most
of these tombs is that they were reopened after the initial
burial or burials and further burials inserted over a period of
several hundred years. It is clear that in many cases the
skeletons which were found in the tombs were incomplete
and it seems that they had previously been placed elsewhere
for a time, perhaps on exposed platforms outside or in
mortuary houses. It is also certain that not all those who died
in this period were buried in the tombs and that some form of
selection was taking place. The scale of the tombs and the
method and length of their use suggest that they were built by
communities rather than individuals. The evidence has been
interpreted as representing a form of ancestor worship, where
relationship to the past was all-important. A further
apparently religious element was that many of the tombs had
entrances facing the rising moon.

Towards the end of the fourth millennium BC there seems
to be evidence for some kind of social instability in more
southerly parts of Britain – areas of cleared woodland
regenerated, tombs were often blocked up and sealed and
there is clear evidence of warfare, although in northern
Scotland there seems to have been less disruption. New types
of communally constructed monuments were built. Known
as henges they were circular enclosures with a ditch around
and a bank inside the ditch (thus they were not defensive)
and either a single entrance or pair of opposed entrances.
Henges seem to have been both symbols of power and also
religious centres; they often developed and changed their
function over long periods of time. At approximately the
same time stone circles begin to be built, a habit which
continued for hundreds of years. Many of these have
survived relatively intact to the present. Their exact function

will remain unknown but it is clear that they were laid out with reference to the important cycles of the sun, although not with the astronomical complexity that is sometimes claimed for them. They are often associated with henges.

Fine examples of both a henge and stone circle were excavated in 1947–48 at Cairnpapple Hill in West Lothian, illustrating the complex development of such sites. The earliest activity took place around 2800 BC and was an arc of seven pits, six containing cremated bone, the remains of five further cremations and possibly a setting of upright stones in the centre of the arc of pits. Subsequently a henge was constructed with an internal area inside the oval bank of 40m by 30m and a ditch 3.5m wide outside. Inside the henge 24 standing stones were erected in an oval, with perhaps a further arrangement of stones in the centre. The only evidence for the existence of the stones appeared to be the holes left after their removal in a later remodelling. The subsequent use of the site is described in the next chapter.

THE EARLY AND MIDDLE BRONZE AGE
c.2500 – 1000 BC

The changes in ritual and burial practice at the end of the Neolithic period represent the first visible signs of a fundamental shift in the organisation of society and its activities. The driving force behind this seems to have been the introduction of metalworking, although its importance as a technique should not be over-stressed as the amount of metalworking carried out was relatively small. From around 2700 BC the first metal artefacts appear in Britain, initially of copper, then of bronze (a harder alloy of copper and tin) and gold. It seems that most of this early material was imported from mainland Europe, where the extraction of copper from ore and the manufacture of tools and weapons had been known for some 2000 years. It is unclear why it took so long for the technology to reach Britain. The earliest metal objects were status symbols, for show, not use. Bronze objects which have been found from the Bronze Age include tools such as axes and knives, weapons such as spears, daggers and rapiers, and objects for personal adornment such as armlets. Flint continued to be used as well to make arrowheads and knives.

From about the same time new forms of pottery vessel appear, known as 'Beakers'. They are tall, elongated vessels with open mouths, often intricately decorated on the outside. They seem to have been associated with the drinking of alcohol, as residues found inside a Beaker from Ashgrove in Fife were chemically analysed and are thought to have been the remains of a sweet mead-like drink, flavoured with honey and herbs. The earliest Beakers are almost always found as grave goods, often in association with a typical group of other objects, such as an archer's wristguard made of stone, fine flint tools and metal daggers. The objects are often unused and made specially for the burial. The burials were inhumations of a single individual, usually under a conspicuous mound of earth or stones and are found all over Europe. In Lothian 'Beakers' have been found accompanying burials in many places, although these burials are generally

12

not covered by mounds. 'Beakers' continued to be made for almost a thousand years.

All these new elements, along with apparent differences in the shape of the skulls of the dead and the belief that the domestic horse had been introduced to Britain at the same time, were interpreted by past archaeologists to be the result of invasion by warriors from the Continent. Re-examination of the evidence and radiocarbon dating have cast doubt on this theory of mass migration. It seems that, while there is an element of migration, the major reason for the spread of the new 'Beaker culture' was in fact the adoption of new ideas and artefact types by local peoples. All the evidence points to Beakers, metalworking and the possession of fine artefacts representing the status symbols of a new society.

The change from communal to individual burial has been interpreted as a change in the organisation of society itself, with the emergence of important local chieftains, associated with the development of tribal and clan loyalties at the expense of the wider community. These chieftains were buried individually, as a sign of their status. In Scotland this burial was generally within a short cist, a rectangular stone box constructed just below ground level. These cists were usually for a single burial, in a crouched position, sometimes with grave goods, although some multiple burials and cremations are known. As well as Beakers, burials were sometimes accompanied by vessels known as 'Food Vessels' which were squat, wide-mouthed pots which may have contained some kind of food offering, although there is as yet no definite proof of this. Some of the cists were covered with a stone cairn or earth mound, of varying size. Often further burials were made later into the upper part of the mound.

These cist and cairn monuments are the commonest surviving monument of this period in Lothian. Cairns tend to survive only in the upland areas where farming is less intensive. They are placed in spectacularly prominent positions, such as those on Sparleton Edge, East Lothian and Carnethy Hill in the Pentlands, emphasising the personal glory of the dead. In the lower-lying areas the mounds, which generally would have been built of earth, have usually been levelled by agriculture and appear only as cropmarks on aerial photographs. Other cists, which may have had no covering mound, are often found during ploughing when the massive capstone is dislodged by the tractor. Many are known from Lothian.

These cairns and barrows were part of a wider ritual landscape which involved stone circles, standing stones and cup-and-ringed marked stones (a form of rock art using symbols). The monuments of the past generations also played a part in this landscape. All the elements were linked together, often in linear arrangements. The significance and rituals involved are difficult to understand. It is certain that astronomy played a part in the process, but not to the extravagant extent which is claimed by some archaeologists and others.

The henge at Cairnpapple in West Lothian illustrates the likely changed significance of the old monuments to the new society. Within the circle of stones erected towards the end of the Neolithic period, a burial with a Beaker was found during excavations, close to the foot of one of the stones. Subsequently a small cairn was built, with a standing stone at its west end; beneath it, a grave pit contained a single inhumation with two Beakers. Later a large cairn of stones was built over two cist burials, one of which contained a Food Vessel. Some of the stones of the stone circle had to be removed to make room for this cairn, 13m in diameter. The cairn was subsequently enlarged to 30m across and two cremations in urns buried within it. Finally, and probably much later, four more burials were inserted into the mound. This complex sequence of activity illustrates the changing role of the holy site in the eyes of the local inhabitants.

The cremations excavated at Cairnpapple also show the move towards cremation in the later part of the period, with the remains often buried in urns, sometimes in groups inside small cemeteries surrounded by a low bank, or inserted into earlier burial monuments.

Elsewhere in Lothian there is a particular concentration of ritual and burial sites around the headwaters of the Whiteadder in the Lammermuirs, in the form of stone circles and cairns. The reasons are unknown, although the route is one of the main ways south across the Lammermuirs. The stone circles themselves are unspectacular small rings of low stones. That on Kingside Hill has a small cairn, probably a later addition, inside the circle. The eastern part of East Lothian, at a lower level, has a concentration of another type of monument of this period, the individual standing stone. These are often massive monolithic blocks which have been variously interpreted as territorial or way markers, astronomical indicators or grave markers. The current distribution is patchy, as many have been removed for building stone or as part of field clearance, making interpretation of those that remain problematical.

The standing stone at Easter Broomhouse has cup-marks carved into its west side. These marks are decoration of patterns of rings, spirals and cups, often found in elaborate arrangements, pounded into the face of stone slabs, upright stones or exposed rock faces. Sometimes stones with these marks were built into the structure of stone burial cists. Their meaning is unclear, although their circular form obviously has links to the other circular monuments of the period.

Unfortunately, despite the relative abundance of ritual and burial monuments of this period evidence for the associated settlements is lacking. The distribution of known sites elsewhere in Britain shows that the period between 2000 and 1500 BC saw a rapid expansion in the area cleared of woodland, even upland areas, presumably for stock-rearing. It seems unlikely, given the obvious presence of people in Lothian, that a similar process did not happen. Most of the country was brought into agricultural production and settlement must have expanded also. Usually these settlements were small groups of buildings, made of the local materials which in Lothian would have been timber, clay and thatch, none of which survive the thousands of years well. In other parts of Scotland, where stone was used for at least the footings of these buildings, impressive groups of round-houses and cairns (probably from clearance of fields for cultivation) have been found, apparently dating to the second millennium BC. Further fieldwork in Lothian may well reveal similar sites.

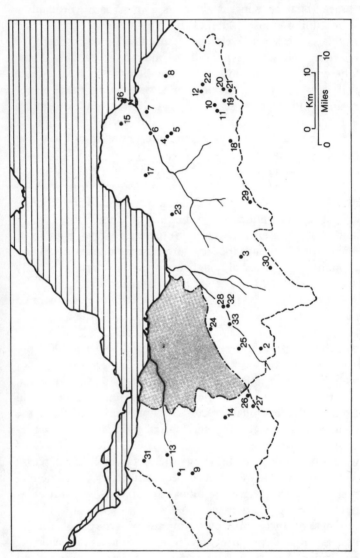

1. Late Neolithic Bronze Age Sites

Late Neolithic Bronze Age Sites

1.   * **Cairnpapple Hill WL**
     NS 987 717

On top of Cairnpapple Hill, 1.5 miles ESE of Torphichen, these monuments are displayed following their excavation. Five phases of activity have been identified, with the earliest a cremation ceremony of around 2800 BC, with a possible setting of upright stones in the centre of the arc of cremation pits. Later a henge was constructed with an area inside an oval bank of 40m by 30m, and a ditch 3.5m wide outside. Inside the henge 24 standing stones were erected in an oval, with perhaps a further arrangement of stones in the centre. A cairn was erected in the circle, probably c.1800-1700 BC, with two cist burials, one with a stone bearing cup-marks. Part of the stone circle was taken down to accommodate the cairn. Subsequently a larger cairn 30m in diameter was built over the smaller cairn, and two cremations in urns buried in pits inside. Four burials of probable Iron Age date were found just beyond the E ditch. Historic Scotland

Standing stones

2.   * **Auchencorth ML**
     NT 204 576

The Gowk Stone is a standing stone in a field 730m E of Auchencorth Farm, 2m high. An inscription on its SE face is thought to be relatively recent.

3.   * **Wright's Houses ML**
     NT 364 606

A standing stone, 1.3m high, on the summit of the ridge, 250m SE of Wright's Houses.

4.   * **Standingstane Farm, Traprain EL**
     NT 577 736

A large standing stone, 2.75m high, stands within the main complex of farm buildings on the S side of the road.

5.   * Cairndinnis Farm EL
NT 578 742

A standing stone, 2.45m high, known as the Loth Stone. Supposedly the burial place of the mythical King Loth, it has been moved from its original location to the edge of the field. Excavation at the time of its removal showed nothing of interest.

6.   * Pencraig Hill EL
NT 581 768

Standing stone, just N of the A1, between Haddington and East Linton, on the slope of Pencraig Hill 3m high, the stone is a three-sided pillar.

7.   * Kirklandhill Farm EL
NT 616 776

A standing stone, 3m high, just N of the A1 at its junction with the A198, now rather forlorn in the middle of the field.

8.   * Easter Broomhouse EL
NT 680 766

Lying S of the farm, a sandstone pillar c. 3m high has cup-marks visible on its W side. The grooves visible at the bottom of the stone were made by a steam plough cable.

9.   Bathgate WL
NS 988 695 and 987 698

A pair of standing stones on the ridge of the hill N of the road between Bathgate and Bangour Hospital. One is 1.5 m high, the other, 70m to the N, is a re-erected stump of a stone.

Stone circles

10.   * Kingside Hill EL
NT 627 650

A circle of 30 small stones, c.12m in diameter, in open moorland on the NW side of the hill, N of the B6355 between Gifford and Cranshaws. Many of the stones are set on their edge but some have fallen and are almost buried.

Inside the circle, the low mound 3m in diameter, with a boulder on top, is probably a burial cairn.

11. * Mayshiel EL
NT 617 646
This stone circle lies only 10m from the S side of the B6355 5.5 miles ESE of Gifford. It is very easy to visit, but is not marked on the Ordnance Survey maps. Seven stones, surrounding a hollowed interior *c.*3m in diameter, are encircled by a low bank.

12. * Yadlee EL
NT 654 673
Located above West Burn, 300m SE of Yadlee, on NE foot of Spartleton Edge. Seven small stones, six of which are still earthfast, lie on the circumference of a circle 8m in diameter.

Cairns

13. * Riccarton Hills WL
NT 018 737
A turf covered cairn, 10-11m diameter, 1.5m high, with a kerb of small boulders around its base is situated on top of the hill, E of Beecraigs Country Park.

14. * Corston Hill WL
NT 087 635
A cairn on the W end of hill above Morton Reservoir is 15m by 17.5m by 1.6m high.

15. * Whitekirk Hill EL
NT 595 819
On the summit of Whitekirk Hill is a cairn, measuring 19m by 17m by 2m high. It is reputed to be the grave of two Covenanters killed by soldiers from the Bass Rock 1670-80, but this is unlikely.

16. * Tyne Mouth EL
NT 637 813

A cairn on a pronounced rocky promontory on N side of the mouth of the River Tyne, measures 18m in diameter, and 3m high.

17. * Gallows Hill EL
NT 506 777

A cairn surviving as a flat mound 20m by 17m by 2m high.

18. * Harestone Hill EL
NT 567 623

Known as Whitestone Cairn, it stands on the summit of one of Lammermuirs, 505m above sea level. Circular, it is 12.5m in diameter and 1m high.

19. * Penshiel Hill EL
NT 637 635

A cairn, 350m above sea level on the NE shoulder of Penshiel Hill, is 10m in diameter at its base, with a flat top 7m in diameter. It rises to $c.$1m above the bottom of a surrounding ditch which is 7m wide. Outside this is a low bank about 2m wide.

20. * Spartleton EL
NT 653 655

The cairn, magnificently situated on the summit of Spartleton, 15m in diameter has some peripheral modern disturbance but is apparently intact otherwise.

21. * Priestlaw Hill EL
NT 652 623

A cairn, 410m above sea level, on the summit of the hill, is 13m in diameter and 1.5m high.

22. * Crystal Rig EL
NT 665 673

Known as the Witches' Cairn, the cairn is 18m in diameter, 1.1m high, with a surveyor's cairn on top.

23. Macmerry EL
NT 435 730

In a field to the S of the A1, just W of the Macmerry junction, is an elongated mound which may be a barrow. A black soilmark is conspicuously visible around the mound after ploughing.

24. * Caerketton Hill ML
NT 237 662

The cairn, in a spectacular location on top of the hill with extensive views on three sides, has been robbed of some of its stones but is still 16m in diameter and 1.5m high.

25. * Carnethy Hill ML
NT 204 619

A large, very conspicuous, cairn built of stones on the summit of the hill, 22m across and 2m high. It is now considerably spread but in 1929 it was circular.

26. * East Cairn Hill ML
NT 122 595

This cairn, with commanding views, is 17m diameter by 2m high. A cist found in the cairn contained a barbed and tanged arrowhead and some bone.

27. West Cairn Hill ML
NT 107 584

Robbed of much of its stone, this cairn still survives to 14m diameter and stands 1.10m high.

28. Mountmarle ML
NT 279 637

Little remains except a slight scarp around the S side of a low knoll. In 1913 it measured 17m in diameter by 2m high and had a bell-shaped profile on the W.

29. Soutra Hill ML
NT 459 591

The OS triangulation pillar stands on top of a flat-topped barrow, 8.5m diameter by 0.4m high.

30. Sowburnrig ML
   NT 347 557

Fifty small cairns cover 1.1 hectares of peaty moorland at the
foot of the Moorfoot Hills, 370m SW of Sowburnrig, and are
probably clearance cairns. They vary from 2m to 4m in
diameter and the largest are 0.5m high.

Cup-and-ring marks

31. * Linlithgow/Bonnytoun Farm WL
   NT 008 783

A cup-and-ring marked stone found at Bonnytoun Farm, is
now built into a summerhouse in Linlithgow. Three cups
with two rings around, two cups with one ring and two cups
with radial grooves are visible.

32. * Glencorse ML
   NT 247 626

A fine cup-marked boulder in churchyard of Glencorse
Parish Church has 26 cups, 10 with encircling rings. It was
supposedly found on the hill above the old parish church
(NT 254 630). A second stone is now lost.

33. * Hawthornden ML
   NT 280 632

A complex arrangement of cups, rings, spirals and angular
marks on an almost inaccessible ledge of the cliff on the E
side of River Esk Gorge.

THE LATE BRONZE AGE AND PRE-ROMAN
IRON AGE *c*.1000 BC – 43 AD

From about 1200 BC onwards the upland areas of Britain which had been cleared and settled during the previous thousand years were abandoned. Blanket bog began to form, creating the areas which we now think of as natural moorland and covering the traces of previous settlement. There seem to have been a number of factors involved in this process. The thin soils of the uplands had been exhausted by over-grazing, the climate had deteriorated and the volcano Hekla, off the coast of Iceland, erupted in 1153 BC, probably causing perpetual winter and acid rain in Scotland for a time. The ensuing crop failures and continuing poor weather probably tipped the balance in areas of farmland which must always have been marginal.

The effects on human society of these environmental factors are not difficult to predict, with subsequent pressure on land and food supplies. Much of the archaeological evidence from this period shows this stress. New weapon types, such as the sword and metal shield, were developed, a large number of hoards of bronze artefacts were buried, often in watery locations (most probably for religious reasons) and defences were built around settlements. A much more divided society seems to have developed, with tribal groups under local chieftains growing in importance. Other changes are evident. Feasting (suggested by the introduction of bronze cauldrons) and a love of display seem to have played a large part in the operation of society. Horsemanship grew in importance, with fine decorative harness fittings found from the turn of the millennium onwards. Ironworking, discovered in the Middle East more than a thousand years earlier, came to Britain on a very small scale from around 650 BC and harder, technically superior iron tools and weapons gradually replaced those of bronze.

All these elements are considered to be typical of the Celtic culture which was almost uniform across Europe in the second half of the first millennium BC. The Celts seem to have formed a distinct ethnic group, originating in Central Europe, who spread westwards in a series of migrations. It is clear, however, that many of the characteristic elements of this culture were present in Scotland before the supposed date of arrival of the Celtic warriors. The elements which are considered typical of Celtic culture took a considerable period to evolve, which tends to argue against the idea of a sudden influx. As with earlier major changes it seems that the new society and culture was the result of a complex process of fusion of native and imported elements.

Whatever its origins, this Celtic culture is the first pre-historic society for which we have evidence other than arch-aeological, with written accounts by Greek and Roman historians of the Celtic tribes which they encountered on their northern frontiers and also from the Irish tales and legends, originally oral but later written down. This evidence shows that it was a hierarchical society, based on the tribe, under a chief. In Lothian, by the time of the Roman invasion in the first century AD, the tribe occupying Lothian is recorded as being the Votadini. The tribe was sub-divided into large family groups, headed by noble warriors whose wealth was reckoned in cattle. Below the nobles were freemen farmers and at the lowest level of society were slaves. A distinct, separate class was formed by the men of art, who included craftsmen, doctors, historians, bards, musicians and the archetypal symbol of the Celts, the Druids, priest-lawyers whose true character has been obscured by modern romanticism but who seem to have played a pivotal role in Celtic life and politics.

This period sees a shift in the nature of the archaeological evidence, with settlement sites surviving well, while evidence for ritual and burial becomes more difficult to detect. No large religious sites are known; it is clear from the known festivals of the later Celts of Ireland that the religious calendar was closely linked to agriculture, with festivals of fertility such as Samhain the winter festival at the start of November and Beltane on May 1, when the cattle were led out to graze. The fate of most of the dead of Iron Age Scotland is unknown, although some inhumation burials have been found, such as the multiple burial cist found at Lochend near Dunbar, where 21 skeletons were found in a cist under a cairn. Other sites have produced evidence of inhumation, both in cists and simply in the ground.

The archaeological remains show clearly the move towards a disturbed and fragmented society. The early defended enclosures, known as palisaded enclosures, were formed of upright timbers surrounding a roundhouse or houses. One of these was excavated at Dryburn Bridge near Dunbar and contained at least two houses in the late Bronze Age phase, one of which was substantial. In this area most of the palisaded enclosures would seem to have been built during the later part of the Bronze Age, although there is some evidence that they continued to be built for many hundreds of years. Placed in defensible sites, the remains of many others may well have been hidden under the later hillforts which are plentiful throughout the territory of the Votadini. It is clear from the evidence of sites such as Broxmouth near Dunbar that unenclosed settlement continued as well, as a large timber house dated between 800 and 500 BC, without any defences, was found under the remains of the later hillfort. The excavated site at Broxmouth shows the complex history of such sites. The site of the house was covered by a defended enclosure inside a single rampart. This defensive ring had four further remodellings, with the addition of more ditches and ramparts and complex gateways. Inside the fort the remains of roundhouses were excavated. These round-houses are the universal type of dwelling in this area in the Iron Age.

Hillforts are often seen as the typical site of the Iron Age; large enclosures on hilltops or promontories, surrounded by often massive defensive ramparts and ditches. Inside the hillforts can often be seen the traces of the foundations of roundhouses. The simple identification of these sites as the seats of the tribal chieftains is no longer tenable. It seems that they played a far more complex role in society than simply lordly residences, acting as store areas for the surpluses produced by the tribe and as ritual, ceremonial and social centres. Hillforts also acted as symbols of the power of the

chieftain and the tribe, as imposing monuments in prominent
positions. The nature of Celtic warfare, based on personal
challenge and horsemanship rather than long sieges, makes
the sometimes amazingly elaborate defences seem slightly
ridiculous, although the prized cattle may well have been
moved into the forts at times of unrest. Some forts, such as
Chesters near Drem, a fort with elaborate multiple defences,
are actually overlooked from nearby hills.

In the later part of the pre-Roman period, there seems to
have been large-scale land division; in Lothian the evidence
for these comes in the form a specific type of site, known as
pit-alignments. These consist of long lines of pits running for
several hundred metres, visible only as cropmarks on aerial
photographs. Only one such pit-alignment has been investigated in Lothian, at Eskbank (Midlothian). The excavations
showed the pits to be oval, 2.5m by 1.5m by 0.7m deep. The
soil excavated from them was used to form long linear banks
running alongside the pits. A particular concentration of
these pit alignments are known from around Chesters hillfort,
near Drem, East Lothian and it has been suggested that these
were associated with occupation of the hillfort, and were
boundaries for large-scale stock-rearing, similar to modern
American ranches.

Whatever the exact function of hillforts, they do seem to
be the apex of a pyramid pattern of settlements. In the
countryside surrounding the hillforts was a network of small
farms, where the majority of the population must have lived
and worked. Many of these farms, either single roundhouses
or groups, were also surrounded by banks and ditches,
although it is clear from the scale and position of these sites
that they were not defensive in character. Few of these sites
have survived above ground level but many are known
because the moisture-retentive soils of their infilled ditches
show up very well on aerial photographs. Unenclosed sites
are also known, and these may represent the lowest rank of
settlement, although excavation at the sites of Broxmouth
and Dryburn Bridge amongst others has shown that phases
of enclosure intermingle with phases of open settlement.
These smaller settlements tend to be on the richer lowland

soils, illustrating their main agricultural function. The farmers would have been involved in mixed farming, growing cereals and keeping animals, with sheep playing an important part in the economy. One of these smaller sites, known from aerial photographs, was excavated at St Germains near Tranent before it was destroyed by mining. Three distinct phases of the site's occupation were identified. The earliest was a circular house inside a polygonal bank and ditch; the ditch had been redug six or seven times after it had silted up, showing a considerable length of occupation. The site was next used for a small fort with a larger bank and ditch and then, finally, as an unenclosed village of six to twelve houses, all with cobbled floors surrounded by the post-holes of the upright timbers of the house structure. Roman Samian pottery was found in these later houses, suggesting an occupation lasting into the early centuries AD. Little of this complex information was discernible from the aerial photographs and the site is a useful warning against attempting to identify sites from cropmark evidence alone.

Traprain Law, a striking volcanic plug standing alone in the middle of the East Lothian countryside, is perhaps the most important hillfort in the region. It has been identified as the tribal capital of the Votadini, although it must be said that there is no certain evidence for this, although its size (second in area only to Eildon Hill, Borders) and the remarkable series of finds from the site illustrate its importance. Artefacts found at the site show its importance from the earliest period of prehistory. The top of the hill is circled by a complex series of visible ramparts, which seem to show that the area enclosed grew in size over the centuries, enclosed within a stone-faced rampart wall which is the best-preserved and most visible set of remains on the site. Many hut circles can be seen inside the ramparts, but how many of these would have been in use at any one time, or for what purpose the buildings were used, could only be shown by detailed and careful excavation of large areas of the site.

This pattern of hillforts and associated subordinate settlements was not uniform across Scotland, although the hillfort region does extend up the east coast through Fife and into

southern Grampian. In the north and west there seems far
less of a stratified society, with life based around individual
small settlements. In the last two centuries BC, new types of
fortified structures appear, including the stone-built towers
known as brochs, built from *c.*100 BC onwards and found
almost exclusively in the north and west of Scotland and duns,
small stone-walled forts of the west and south-west, fortified
homesteads which continued in use for many centuries. The
other major type of defended settlement is the crannog, an
artificial island in a loch, usually consisting of a platform
formed of timber piles, with a house built on it, linked by a
causeway to the land. Crannogs were built from early prehistory through to relatively modern times; no definite
examples are known from Lothian outside Edinburgh,
although one is reputed to have been discovered when
Lochcote Loch near Torphichen in West Lothian was drained.

Iron Age Sites

There are many sites from the whole of the late Bronze Age
and the Iron Age which are known only as cropmarks on
aerial photographs and have no physical evidence above
ground level. They are not included in this gazetteer. It
should also be remembered that many of the sites listed here
may well have been occupied into the Roman period
described in the next chapter.

Palisaded enclosures

1.   * **Braidwood ML**
      NT 193 596
Small-scale excavations of this settlement site on the crest of
Camp Hill, 500m N of Braidwood Farm revealed a complex
sequence of structures, including two circuits of palisades
and a pair of ditches with a rampart between. The trench of
the inner palisade is still visible on the ground, enclosing an
area 55m by 35m. The outer palisade, later incorporated in
the rampart, was approximately 13m beyond the inner. Both
palisades had entrances on the SW, although it is not certain

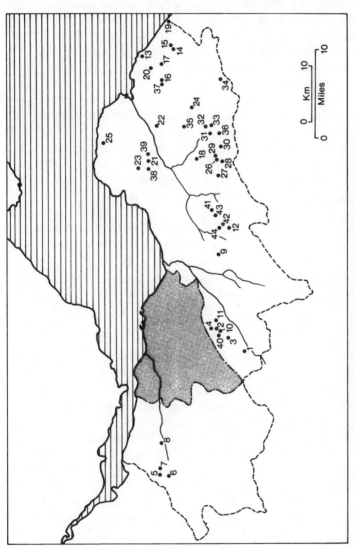

2. The Late Bronze Age and Pre-Roman Iron Age

that they were contemporary. A rampart was built
subsequently, of material dug out to form ditches, with its
entrance also on the SW. Inside are traces of sixteen houses,
mostly of ring-ditch type, although excavation showed some
had rings of posts inside to support the roof structure. Some
of the houses clearly pre-date the inner palisade.

2.   * Castle Knowe ML
     NT 2307 640

A palisaded settlement lying on the shoulder of the hill
overlooking Castlelaw fort. On the N side two palisade
trenches are visible, 6m apart. The interior measures 70m by
30m and at the top of the steep slope on the south the
remains of at least three timber houses are marked by
platforms. Part of the outer palisade is obscured by upcast
from later slit trenches but on the NE side the line is
continued by a low bank with an external ditch. A counter-
scarp bank at its E end may be an unfinished defensive work
or may be to protect the entrance. Rig and furrow cultivation
over the site has obliterated part of the E perimeter. A short
length of ditch and bank lies 30m to the NE.

3.   * Lawhead ML
     NT 216 622

Part of a palisaded enclosure is visible within an earthwork
fort on top of the hill SE of Turnhouse Hill. Roughly circular
originally, 30m in diameter, only the N side is clearly visible.
The earthwork is a fort measuring 85m by 60m within a
rampart and ditch, with the rampart surviving in places 1.7m
above the bottom of the ditch. The defences are badly
scalped on the S of the site by cultivation. Inside the rampart
the remains of nine houses are visible, two especially well
defined, 13m in diameter.

4.   * Woodhouselee Hill ML
     NT 233 650

On the S shoulder of the hill, within the remains of an old
plantation boundary, are remains of an oval palisaded
enclosure, 72m by 50m internally, with entrances on the SE

and possibly the N sides. The perimeter is formed by two sets of double palisade trenches, neither complete.

Forts

5. Bowden Hill WL
NS 978 744

A fort on the E end of the hill, *c.* 1.5 miles NE of Torphichen, consists of a walled enclosure surrounded by a single stone wall. Further features of uncertain function and form are visible within the defences.

6. Castlethorn : Carniewell Slack WL
NS 975 725

A fort, immediately E of Torphichen, on the highest part of the knoll. Surrounded by a low bank up to 2m thick with a second bank on the N taking in a lower terrace. The entrance is to the W, with a trackway leading downhill, marked by two upright stones (NS 9745 7251).

7. *Cockleroy WL
NS 989 744

A fort on the summit of the hill, with a tumbledown stone wall enclosing an area 125m by 60m, with a further wall visible to the NW.

8. Peace Knowe WL
NT 031 741

To the NW of Ochiltree Mill, a fort with triple ramparts on the S and W and double ramparts on the E, measuring 60m by 45m. The entrance is on the W side.

9. Camp Wood Hill ML
NT 360 638

Inside a forestry plantation on the summit of the hill is a fort with a rampart 8.5m wide and 1m high enclosing an area measuring 130m by 110m. Inside several smaller enclosures are visible, some of which lie against the rampart.

10. * Castle Law ML
NT 229 639

A multivallate fort on a spur on the SE side of Castlelaw Hill, 150m NNW of Castlelaw Steading. The fort measures 90m by 45m inside defences formed by a low inner rampart with two outer ditches accompanied by counter-scarp banks. Entrances are visible on the E, S and W sides. Excavations in 1948 showed the ramparts to be built of clay, reinforced with layers of brushwood, vertical stakes and horizontal timbers. At the E entrance a complex sequence of successive gates was uncovered, showing the long history of the site. Inside the fort, after the abandonment of the outer defences, a souterrain was constructed. *Historic Scotland.*

11. Hillend ML
NT 245 662

All that is visible of this fort (measuring 70m by 50m) on a knoll on the NE side of Caerketton Hill is a low rampart on the W and N, with a stretch of an outer ditch with an external bank on the W side, which is the easiest way to approach the fort. A possible house site lies at the S end of the ridge which bisects the interior of the fort.

12. Longfaugh ML
NT 404 618

At 500m W of Longfaugh farmhouse is a substantial fort on a knoll at the E end of a ridge of higher ground. Circular in plan, it measures about 70m in diameter, with two ramparts and a broad ditch between them. A badly damaged entrance on the E is protected by a hornwork from the rampart.

13. Broxmouth EL
NT 701 774

Excavations at what appeared to be a multivallate fort, E of Dunbar, showed a complex history of remains. The earliest occupation was a large circular house, then a fort with two entrances in a single rampart was erected. There were then four major and two minor phases of alteration, with variation of defences between single and double ramparts. There are house sites in the interior, of which five were excavated. A small cemetery of nine inhumations was found outside the fort, with four further loosely-flexed burials inside. Activity on the site was shown to have taken place from 2000 to 1000 BC on a sporadic basis, then more consistently during the whole of the first millennium BC until the second-century AD.

14. Blackcastle Hill EL
NT 713 717 .

The fort on the W end of the hill, over Aikengall Water, is enclosed by stone rampart 52m by 46m, surrounded by a single ditch. At a later date an outer rampart and ditch was begun but never finished, leaving four segments of bank and ditch.

15. Blackcastle Hill EL
NT 721 723

At the E end of the hill lies a ploughed out (but still slightly visible) enclosure, 43m by 33m.

16. The Chesters EL
NT 660 739

About a mile SW of Spott village, this circular bivallate fort, badly damaged by ploughing and robbing, is 107m in diameter with two massive ramparts and external ditches.

17. Brunt Hill EL
NT 690 745

The slight remains of an enclosure, 34m in diameter, are visible as a slight depression with a ploughed-out bank visible on the E and W sides.

18. The Chesters, Eaglescairnie Mains EL
NT 512 687

A large oval fort, 150m by 120m, survives as double ramparts only in the NW and SE corners.

19. Castledykes, Bilsdean EL
NT 766 726

The fort on top of sea-cliffs east of the farm is defended on landward side by a massive earth rampart, enclosing a long triangular area measuring 180m by 78m.

20. Doon Hill EL
NT 683 755

On the shoulder of the hill, $c.$100m W of the summit, are the damaged remains of an oval fort with triple ramparts on E and S sides, measuring 122m by 76m internally.

21. * Kaeheughs EL
NT 518 763

A fort at the E end of the Garleton Hills, $c.$500m W of Barney Mains, which has been quarried away on the E side. The rest is an enclosure inside a substantial stony rampart, covered by two others at wide intervals. The interior has slight hollows which are possibly house sites.

22. * Traprain Law EL
NT 582 748

A massive hilltop stronghold, 17 hectares in area, which is one of the largest in southern Scotland with evidence of occupation on the top of the volcanic plug throughout prehistory. Stray finds of mesolithic flints point to activity in that period, but the earliest substantive occupation found by excavations earlier this century seems to have been in the mid-second millennium BC, when the site was used for burial of cremations in urns. By the end of the Bronze Age there was evidence for buildings, as well as metalworking, with moulds for spears, swords and axes found. It is assumed that the earliest phases of defences, enclosing 4 hectares in ramparts, belong to this period. There is evidence of later occupation during the Iron Age which indicates expansion and contraction of the area. It appears that the hillfort has been enclosed by further ramparts, up to the maximum extent when the most visible rampart at the base of the hill on the N and that enclosing the flat area to the W of the hilltop were built. A later, more massive stone wall high on the N side and apparently overlying the earlier rampart on the W represents a contraction in the size of the hillfort.

23. * Chesters, Drem EL
NT 508 783

A very large (275m by 45m internally) fort with a well-preserved series of complex defences with up to six ramparts and associated ditches visible in places. The interpretation of these as wholly defensive is compromised by the fact that the fort is not on the top of the hill and is, in fact, overlooked. Foundations of huts are visible in the interior, some of which lie over parts of the defences showing continued occupation.

24. * White Castle EL
NT 613 687

Immediately next to the road S through the Lammermuirs and 2 miles SE of Garvald, this fort sits on a steep promontory protected by three ramparts, possibly originally topped with stone walls and is 70m by 40m internally.

25. * North Berwick Law EL
NT 555 842

A spectacularly placed fort has defences about 15m below the summit, with drystone walls enclosing an area c. 150m by 90m and the remains of second and third walls visible on the gentler slope. In the lowest enclosure can be seen outlines of circular house platforms.

26. * Kidlaw EL
NT 512 642

On the E side of the burn 300m E of the farm, is a fine circular fort, 110m in diameter inside three ramparts with external ditches, with entrances on W and E sides. Traces of earlier defences are visible in the SE part.

27. * Stobshiel EL
NT 497 638

A promontory fort on a plateau in an angle of Birns Water

with good natural defences enhanced by a stony rampart enclosing a roughly triangular area (58m by 76m), with entrances in the NW and NE. An outer rampart 15m beyond the inner has a wide defensive ditch, 9m wide with another rampart 9m thick and 4.5m high

28. * Witches Knowe EL
NT 519 635

East of the reservoir, 3 miles SSW of Gifford, lies a fort with three ramparts. The innermost is 3.5 thick and made of stone; the outer ramparts have ditches. There are entrances to the fort on the SW and SE.

29. * The Castles, Dumbadam Burn EL
NT 531 642

An oval fort, 2.5 miles S of Gifford, multivallate, 90m by 45m, sits on an outcrop above the burn with a poorly preserved inner rampart inside a ditch which was only dug where necessary, with an entrance at each end. Outside a further rampart lies *c.* 30m away, with further defences visible to the N and W.

30. * Harelaw EL
NT 546 632

A substantial fort 3 miles SE of Gifford, on a spur between two burns was protected by a timber-laced wall 4m thick, with evidence for vitrification. It is now extensively robbed. Further defences are visible on the NW and SE sides, and on the SW two ramparts and ditches cut off access, leaving only a narrow causeway for access.

31. * Park Burn EL
1. NT 571 652
2. NT 573 655

1. Three ramparts and external ditches surround an enclosure 59m by 58m which is 2.75 miles SE of Gifford. The inner rampart is badly damaged; the best-preserved stretch of defences are on the SW side.
2. A much damaged fort 400m NE of 1. above, with a

rampart 5m wide and 0.6m high visible on W, S and E sides.

32. * Black Castle EL
NT 580 662
In woodland 3 miles SE of Gifford lies an almost circular fort with two ramparts with a ditch between. The inner rampart is 6m high in places and has a stone wall on top, an apparently local characteristic element of fort defences.

33. * Green Castle EL
NT 582 657
A triangular fort on the right bank of Newlands Burn, 3.25 miles SE of Gifford with two ramparts enclosing an area 70m by 58m.The inner rampart is enhanced by its position on the edge of the plateau; the second rampart outside is less substantial.

34. Friar's Nose EL
NT 664 632
A well-preserved multivallate fort, 8.5 miles ESE of Gifford, on a promontory over the Whiteadder Water with four ramparts, possibly representing two phases of construction.

35. * Garvald Mains EL
NT 583 698
A circular fort 0.75 miles S of Garvald, sits on a plateau above the Papana Water. A wide rampart with stone wall on its upper surface encloses an area 85m by 73m.

36. * The Hopes EL
NT 570 636
A large fort, 2.25 hectares at its largest extent, 3.5 miles SE of Garvald, of multi-period construction. A complex series of remains of ramparts and ditches, at the centre of which is a triple rampart enclosure 106m by 75m. Below the fort on the E are cross-ridge dykes 10m wide and 2m high.

37. * The Chesters EL
NT 660 739

A circular fort, 140m in diameter, inside two massive
ramparts with external ditches. These impressive remains lie
2.5 miles E of Stenton.

38. Skid Hill EL
NT 507 764

A fort is visible on a terrace on the W side of the hill as a wall
3m wide and 0.3m high. An inner rampart is visible as a
slight rise 7m uphill.

39. Seaton Law EL
NT 533 766

A large fort (190m by 76m) with four ditches, the inner of
which encloses a sub-rectangular area lies on the top of
Hanging Craig above Athelstaneford.

Unenclosed settlements

40. Castlelaw Hill ML
NT 222 641

A ring-ditch visible on the spur projecting from the foot of
Castlelaw Hill immediately W of the rifle range is a house
platform 12m in diameter, with a ditch up to 2.5m wide,
formed of shallow scoops.

Scooped settlements

41. Brotherstone Hill ML
NT 436 553

A possible scooped homestead on the S slope of the hill,
800m NE of Nether Brotherstone, is cut into the hill and
enclosed by a stone and earth bank up to 5m thick. Two
possible houses are visible in the interior.

42. Longfaugh ML
NT 411 618

A shallow scoop 65m by 45m 200m E of the steading is

visible, with an enclosing ditch recorded on aerial photographs.

43. Nether Brotherstone ML
1. NT 431 547
2. NT 429 551

1. A possible scooped homestead lies on the SE slope, measuring 21m by 17m with traces of a bank around it.

2. On the W face of the hill, a scooped settlement overlies the remains of an earlier earthwork which measured 110m by 75m within a bank and ditch which have been much obliterated by the construction of the settlement.

44. Preston Mains ML
NT 407 653

Cropmarks show a circular ditched enclosure (60m in diameter) with an internal scoop about 40m in diameter visible on the ground.

THE ROMAN IRON AGE
43 – 410 AD

The period of substantial Roman presence in Scotland totals less than 40 years, but it has left behind some of the most enduring and extensively (perhaps disproportionately) explored archaeological remains in the country. In contrast the contemporary sites of the Celtic tribes have been little investigated, particularly in south-east Scotland and much of the relationship between the Roman invader and the native population has to be inferred.

The Roman emperor Claudius arrived with his army on the south-east coast of Britain in AD 43. During the following 35 years the south and midlands of England were pacified and Romanised. It was not until AD 78 that the Romans felt secure enough to move north to attempt to conquer the rest of the country, with the first of three major campaigns into Scotland.

The first advance came with the appointment of a new governor of the province of Britannia, Gnaeus Julius Agricola, whose campaigns were recorded by his son-in-law, the historian Tacitus. The march north began in either AD 79 or AD 80, with rapid progress made through northern England into southern Scotland with a two-pronged invasion to isolate the tribe of the Selgovae who lived in upper Tweeddale; in the east the army seems to have advanced via the territory of the Votadini, through Lauderdale, over Soutra Hill and down to cross the North Esk near Dalkeith, continuing north before crossing the Forth near Stirling.

The line of this invasion route has been postulated on the basis of its later consolidation as the major Roman road, Dere Street, much of whose course is still followed by the A68 and which remains one of the most obvious and enduring monuments to the Roman presence, still used for its original purpose of arterial communication. A second Roman road from the west runs along the south side of the Pentlands to join it near Eskbank. Fine sections of these Roman roads can be seen at Carlops and Eight Mile Burn, as well as over the top of Soutra Hill in Midlothian.

Agricola's advance to the north was rapid, reaching the Tay estuary in a single season. The speed of this advance demonstrates clearly that the Romans must have felt secure to their rear. In Lothian this security seems to have been the result of friendly relations with the Votadini. They did not establish a network of forts to guard their supply lines or to subjugate the native population as they did in other areas. The only permanent large fort known to have been established in Lothian at this time was placed to guard the bridgehead at Elginhaugh (NT 322 673) near Dalkeith. Discovered by aerial photography, it was extensively excavated during 1986 and shown to be the base for a mixed force of infantry and cavalry. The only other site of any permanence which might be attributed to this period is the enigmatic small fortlet at Castle Greg, with room for a small garrison of 160 men. Lying on moorland in the heart of the Pentlands it was never served by a road.

Even in the later periods of Roman occupation no forts are known within this northern part of Votadinian territory to the east of Inveresk at Musselburgh (occupied during the second century occupation only). Several sites of Roman military marching camps, erected during campaigns as temporary fortified enclosures and then levelled as the army moved on, are known from aerial photography. Of varying size, they probably relate to distinct campaigns and are generally found in Lothian along the main lines of invasion and communication. It is not yet possible to allocate securely the different sizes of camp to separate campaigns.

After the end of the governorship of Agricola, Roman withdrawal from much of Scotland was relatively rapid, with the conquest incomplete and Elginhaugh appears to have been demolished by AD 87. The Romans did not completely abandon their Votadinian allies; forts such as Newstead near Melrose were maintained for a further ten years or so, acting as bases for patrols to the north and a bulwark against trouble from less pliant tribes.

The Romans only returned in any strength to Scotland in the years following the accession of the emperor Antoninus

Pius, who, through his governor Quintus Lollius Urbicus, established a new frontier between the Firth of Forth and Firth of Clyde from AD 140. The Antonine Wall, which replaced Hadrian's Wall as the north-western frontier of the Roman Empire, was in fact a massive earth and timber rampart, protected on its north side by a ditch and garrisoned by a large number of forts and fortlets built into its length. The eastern terminus of the wall lay just beyond Lothian at Carriden. Further east the Romans built permanent forts on the coast at Cramond and Inveresk as part of an extended defensive system, to prevent outflanking moves by sea by hostile tribes to the north.

Again the Votadini seem to have caused no trouble to the Roman occupiers and indeed it seems that there was a general acceptance of the alliance with the Romans. On many of the native Votadinian sites which have been excavated or where finds have been collected, Roman artefacts are often found – imported pottery, coins, jewellery, brooches and other items. Closer analysis of the distribution of these finds has suggested that they in fact only occur on native sites of higher status and may well, in fact, represent prestige goods offered to the tribal leadership by the Romans in return for their continued support. For the majority of the population life seems to have continued as before the arrival of the Romans, with little disruption to the settlement of the area. It is difficult, without further excavation, to assign occupation of native sites to this period. Many of the sites which are listed in the previous chapter are as likely to have been occupied at some stage during the Roman period. It is impossible to ascertain the date of the sites known from cropmarks. One particular new type of site may be securely linked with this period – souterrains. Souterrains are stone-built underground structures, often with long passages and chambers built into them. They are found over a wide area of Scotland during the first three centuries AD, but mainly in the north and east. Their function is uncertain, but they may have acted as secure stores for foodstuffs. Some are associated with houses, others seem to stand alone.

Excavations and aerial photography at Inveresk have

shown it to be a place of some importance. The fort itself was a standard Roman establishment, apparently housing a cavalry unit of 500. Outside the defences of the fort, however, a *vicus*, or semi-urban settlement, developed around the fort, covering an area of 10 hectares. Some of the houses were stone-built and had hypocaust heating systems. Further away from the fort an organised and regular field system was laid out. The local population must have been drawn by the opportunity to trade and provide services to the Roman army, but other evidence suggests something of the official involvement of the Roman Government in the origins of the *vicus*. Two inscriptions from Inveresk show the presence of a Roman procurator, or civilian administrator, called Quintus Lucius Sabinianus, in the area. This can only be linked with the establishment of an organised Roman administration of the area on a peaceful rather than military basis, perhaps with an eye on the rich agricultural lands of East Lothian. These occurrences show clearly, but on a limited basis, the interaction between the Romans and the Votadini during this period, a process which in the south of England led to the full assimilation of the native population into the Roman imperial system and culture. At Inveresk the process ceased with the abandonment of the fort *c.*160 AD, when the Antonine Wall was abandoned. Again the Romans maintained a presence in southern Scotland, undoubtedly partially to ensure the security of the Votadini.

In the early 3rd-century the Romans tried again to conquer Scotland, led by the emperor Septimius Severus from AD 208. The evidence suggests that the advance was made straight north along Dere Street, through Lothian and onwards, north of the Forth into Tayside and southern Grampian. Inveresk was not reoccupied, although Cramond (Edinburgh) was; it possessed one of the few easily accessible harbours on the east coast and was used as a supply base for the campaigns north of the Forth, not as an outpost fort of the Antonine Wall which was not reoccupied. The campaigns of the emperor were brief. He died at York in AD 211 and it appears that his successor, his son Caracalla, who had accompanied him on the Scottish campaigns, almost immediately withdrew from Scotland, back to the line of Hadrian's Wall. The Romans did not attempt to conquer Scotland again.

It is clear that the importance of the Votadini as an ally became greater after the Roman withdrawal, with the tribe acting as a buffer between Romanised Britain and the increasingly hostile tribes further north. How the alliance operated is unclear. What is certain is that the Roman empire came under severe and growing pressure on many of its borders, including Britain, from invading tribes. From Ireland into western Scotland came the Scots, who allied themselves with the tribes of the north, known to the Romans as the Picts (literally 'the painted ones'). They began hostile raids into southern Scotland and northern England, presumably attacking the Votadini as well, raids which culminated in the great 'Barbarian Conspiracy' of AD 367 when the Picts, Scots and seaborne Saxons allegedly launched concerted attacks on the province of Britannia, although the extent of the troubles may have been exaggerated for Roman propaganda purposes.

A clue to the turmoil of this period is given by a spectacular discovery made on Traprain Law in 1919 when a hoard of more than 100 pieces of fine Roman silver was uncovered by a workman. It included flagons, bowls, wine strainers and other decorative pieces. A coin of the emperor Honorius who ruled between AD 395 and 423 shows the date of the hoard. The silver had been flattened and cut up and then buried, showing that it was valued as bullion rather than as art. The reasons for its presence within the fort cannot be proved – it may have been booty from a raid, payment for the services of the Votadini by the Romans, or a bribe to the local chieftain to keep the Votadini out of the war. Whatever the reason, it was the reign of Honorius which saw the Roman authorities leave Britain to its own fate.

Roman Sites

Forts

1. Elginhaugh ML
NT 321 673

A fort, discovered by aerial photography but subsequently destroyed by development. Excavation showed it to be of Flavian date, linked with the campaigns of Agricola (*c.* AD 80–87). It was built on the bank of the North Esk on top of a steep scarp, 250m N of Elginhaugh Bridge, to accommodate some 720 infantry and 120 cavalry within a fort with an area of 1.26 hectares internally. It was protected by three or four ditches around a rampart 6–8m thick. All buildings were of timber except a single workshop. An annexe on the west side had been used for a variety of purposes, including drying grain and, subsequently, cooking ovens. Coin evidence suggests it was abandoned by AD 87.

The bath-house of the fort (NT 3212 6718) probably lay within a defended annexe. It measures 23m by 7.5m and is divided into three square rooms with a projecting apse at the W end. Trial excavations showed it to survive to 1.1m high, with 11 courses of masonry.

2. Inveresk EL
NT 345 721

Excavations have shown that a Roman fort lies in the area around St Michael's Church on the top of the bluff formed by the River Esk. Two phases of occupation in the Antonine period were identified. It has been suggested that the fort was the base for a cavalry regiment of 500 men. To the east of the fort, along the gravel ridge, remains of a substantial civilian settlement with stone buildings have been found, including a possible pottery-making site. Part of a hypocaust heating system survives in the grounds of Inveresk House. The possible location of the fort cemetery was discovered in the valley below when skeletons were found in Brunton's Wireworks in 1985 along the projected line of Roman road out of the fort. A regular field system to the south, associated with the occupation of the fort, is known from aerial photographs.

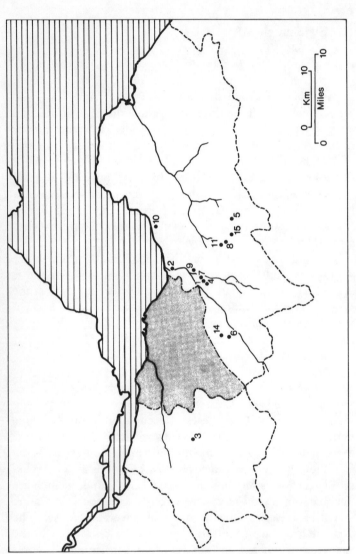

3. Roman Sites

3. * **Castle Greg WL**
    NT 050 592

One of the best preserved Roman earthworks in the country, and one of the first ever excavated (by Sir Daniel Wilson in the 19th-century). It measures 38m x 50m with a rampart 5m thick which rises 0.9m above the level of the interior and about 1.8m above the bottom of the innermost of the two surrounding ditches. On the N side of the entrance the rampart rises for a distance of 6m towards the interior, perhaps to give access to the top of the rampart. A circular depression visible inside is a well excavated by Wilson to a depth of 3.4m.

Temporary camps

Known from aerial photographs only.

4. **Eskbank ML**
    NT 321 668

Two superimposed camps visible on aerial photographs on the N side of the Esk opposite Elginhaugh, now largely covered by housing developments.

5. **Fala Mill ML**
    NT 431 619

150m N of Fala Mill, the S corner and 120m of the SE side of a temporary camp can be identified from cropmarks.

6. **Flotterstone ML**
    NT 233 627

Parts of NE and SE sides of a temporary camp show on an aerial photograph on the SE side of the A702.

7. **Lugton ML**
    NT 325 674

A small temporary camp, only 0.6 hectares can be identified by aerial photography 200m N of Elginhaugh fort.

8.   Pathhead ML
NT 39 63

Three camps in fields to the S of Pathhead. Immediately S of village is a camp of 20.5 hectares with, in the E part of its interior, a smaller camp of 5.3 hectares. The SE ends of both these camps are cut across by the NW angle of a third camp which probably enclosed c.66 hectares and which is probably of Severan date.

9.   Smeaton ML
NT 343 690

Cropmarks show the line of the SE and SW sides of a temporary camp.

10. Spittal ML
NT 471 780

Air survey shows cropmarks of at least one, and probably two, camps, 450m SSE of Spittal steading. Trial trenching in 1985 showed that the larger camp encloses 16.9 hectares and pre-dates the road which runs across SE flank of the Pentlands.

11. Woodhead ML
NT 384 638

Aerial photographs have revealed a complex group of temporary structures SE of Woodhead Farm, including a small camp of 1.5 hectares on the crest of a promontory, with a polygonal outer work enclosing a further 6 hectares on the N and W sides. Other ditches are visible to the E and NE of the smaller camp, but are of uncertain relationship. The complex is probably Flavian (late 1st-century AD) and for a specialised but unknown purpose.

Roads

12. * Dere Street ML

The main Roman road on the east side of lowland Scotland runs from Lauderdale into Midlothian on the Armet Water (NT 4542 5751). The road can be seen for 75m as an *agger* (embankment) mounting a steep slope before disappearing in hollow tracks of more recent date. It seems to follow the main track, with quarry pits on its W side as far as Beatman's Acre, past Soutra Aisle and down the hill, lying below or parallel to the A68, past the temporary camps at Fala Mill and Pathhead. It crosses the Tyne at Ford, near the temporary camp at Woodhead before disappearing. It certainly crosses the North Esk at Elginhaugh, near Dalkeith where a section cut across the road E of Elginhaugh fort in 1980 showed an agger of sand, pebbles and gravel 9.5 metres wide, with ditches 1.5m and 0.3m deep. The line of the road on aerial photographs runs W towards the line of the A7 which is thought to be the line of the Roman road towards Liberton.

13. * Pentlands Road ML
The course of the Roman road along the S side of the Pentlands from Carlops to Glencorse is followed by the A702 and the old turnpike road. At Spittal the temporary camp pre-dates the road. At 1.5km NE of the camp, the line of the road is visible along the ridge to the E of the Pillar Knowe, with quarry pits visible on its N side (NT 1836 5868 to 1905 5918). The route then coincides with the turnpike road and the A702 from Silverburn. It is uncertain where it is heading after this – perhaps to Elginhaugh in the Flavian period and Inveresk in the Antonine period.

Souterrains

14. Castle Law ML
NT 229 638
A souterrain was found in the hollow of the inner ditch on the S side of the E entrance, constructed after the outer defences had been abandoned. Measuring 17m long, between 1 and 2m wide it terminates in a corbelled apse at the S end. The entrance is at the N, with a short passage off the W side, leading into a beehive chamber. Finds from the souterrain included an enamelled brooch, a Romano-Celtic mount, fragments of Roman bottle-glass and Samian pottery, all from the 2nd-century AD.

15. ⋆ Crichton Mains ML
     NT 400 619

On the N side of a low ridge 300m WNW of the fort at Longfaugh. The well-preserved curved chamber is 15.7m long, tapering from 2m to 1.5m wide. The lintel of a possible entrance lies at the NW end. The walls of the chamber and side passage contain Roman carved stones and one of the original eight lintels of the chamber appears to bear the carving of Pegasus, the symbol of the Second Legion Augusta. The Roman stone probably came from a nearby Roman military installation, the location of which is now unknown.

EARLY HISTORIC PERIOD
*c.*410 – 1100 AD

The centuries which followed the end of the Roman government of southern Britain have been known as the 'Dark Ages' because of the lack of detailed knowledge about the period. As in prehistory, much of the evidence is archaeological and even this is very fragmentary. Some flesh on the bare bones is provided by a heroic poem, *The Gododdin*, which tells of the heroes of the tribe (the Votadini) in their unsuccessful war against the Angles of Northumbria who began to expand northwards from the later part of the 6th century. The unsettled times seem to have accentuated the heroic elements in the British Celtic society, with the lord's hall and feasting at the core of social life described in the epic poems. Pastoralism seems to have become the dominant agricultural force, instead of arable farming; horse-riding and associated skills were glorified. Craftsmanship remained important, with evidence for a variety of industries, especially metalworking and the carving of stone and bone in artistic fashion, all linked to a love of personal display. Pottery disappears from the archaeological record with the exception of a few, high status, imported finewares. Pottery vessels were presumably replaced by wood and leather containers and metal cauldrons were used for cooking (although much meat was roasted).

It is generally held that the troubles of the post-Roman period saw the refortification of hilltops, albeit on a smaller scale, with the creation of small 'nuclear' forts or citadels, the strongholds of local leaders. These were far smaller than the large defensive circuits of the earlier part of the Iron Age and were often enclosed within stone wall ramparts. There is little certainty as to which sites in Lothian were the centres of power, with little evidence for the occupation of Traprain Law beyond the early 5th-century. It is possible that the centre of power of the tribe shifted west; a fine stone-walled fort is known on Dalmahoy Hill in Edinburgh; and it has been suggested that there were similar citadels on Arthur's

Seat and the Castle Rock in Edinburgh as well as at the
Castle Rock of Stirling.

The social upheaval of these centuries was accompanied
by the introduction of a new religion, although there is little
physical evidence for its practice in Lothian. Christianity was
the state religion of the later Roman Empire and, while the
manner of its survival and spread after the end of the Roman
administration is unclear, it is generally believed that the
British kingdoms of southern Scotland converted to
Christianity in the 5th and 6th centuries. The most
convincing evidence for the spread of the new religion in
Lothian is the introduction of a new burial rite, inhumation
within a stone cist. These long cists are similar in construction to the short cists of the Bronze Age. They were
larger, as they contained a single body, lying full length.
There were no grave goods accompanying the burials. Often
they are found grouped in cemeteries of up to 200 individuals. These are interpreted as Christian burials because
they are inhumations (cremation was not allowed by the
church) generally aligned east-west in the Christian tradition
and because some had marker stones with inscriptions in
Latin, the language of the church. Such a cemetery was
excavated around the Catstane, in western Edinburgh. A
large cemetery was excavated on England's Hill at Parkburn
(ML NT 2986 6733 to 2998 6744) in advance of quarrying.
One hundred and eleven cists were excavated in 1954 and
1956, all aligned approximately east-west. There was
evidence for two distinct groups of cists, separated by a wall
along the crest of the hill. One group were well-built and
widely spaced; the others were built of less substantial stones
and showed evidence of disturbance and successive construction. A further six cists were excavated in 1962 and one
contained carved Roman stones, including three arch
voussoirs, presumably from the Roman fort at Elginhaugh
near Dalkeith. The division in the cemetery may be evidence
of a differentiation of social class.

Long cist cemeteries are found throughout Lothian,
although generally in the lower-lying areas, which indicate the
presence of widespread settlement. However, while it can be

assumed that the cemeteries must lie close to settlements very little is known at present about the settlements themselves. A clue to their character is provided by the site excavated at Doon Hill, near Dunbar. Here a timber hall was built inside a defensive palisade during the 6th century. The hall was rectangular, in contrast to the traditions of more than 1500 years of round-houses, with protruding V-shaped gable ends. It was 23m long, built of timber and had a large chamber at the centre with smaller rooms at each end.

This hall at Doon Hill was replaced later in time by another built in a different style. The replacement, again built within the defensive palisade, was a large aisled hall with buttresses almost identical in plan to the palace of the 7th-century Anglian King Edwin at Yeavering in Northumberland. During the later part of the 6th century the power of the Anglian kingdom of Bernicia, the northern part of the large kingdom of Northumbria, had grown and in the first half of the 7th century the Anglians moved north and took control of much of southern Scotland. Edinburgh fell to King Oswald in AD 638. The advance of the Anglians was only halted by the power of the Picts to the north in the later part of the century, with the defeat of the Northumbrian army at the battle of Nechtansmere in 685. Lothian, however, remained part of Northumbria for more than three centuries.

The physical evidence for the Anglians in the area of occupation is very limited and the relationship between invader and native even less well known. The place-name evidence shows clearly the extent of settlement with unambiguously Anglian names common in East Lothian, such as Morham, Whittinghame, Tyninghame, Oldhamstocks, and Athelstaneford; other places kept their Celtic names despite evidence of substantial Anglian occupation, such as Dunbar, where an Anglian settlement has been excavated or Aberlady, where Anglian artefacts have been found in considerable quantity. It seems unlikely that there was immigration of Anglian settlers on any massive scale, rather it was the settlement of the aristocracy and their supporters, along with a new culture, law and systems of landholding which brought about changes in Lothian. The place-name evidence suggests that the incomers established a network of unenclosed villages and settlements, many of which remain in the same locations today. Such continuity helps to explain the absence of physical evidence for the settlements of this period, as their remains lie beneath the modern villages.

Within the Anglian kingdom Christianity continued to flourish, and the clearest reminders of the Anglian presence in Lothian are the fragments of fine carved stone crosses from Abercorn, Aberlady and Morham. A bishopric and monastery were established at Abercorn in West Lothian before AD 685. A monastery was in existence at Tyninghame by the mid-9th century but may date to a century earlier, possibly during the lifetime of St Baldred. There are differing and contradictory accounts of the life of the saint, even the century when he was ministering to the peoples of Lothian is uncertain, but his name has survived in many places of religious significance in the northern part of East Lothian around North Berwick and Tyninghame, where his cell was alleged to have been.

The monasteries of this period are very different from the better known examples of the medieval period. They were usually large circular enclosures with banks around, with a church or chapel at the core with individual cells for the monks. Outside the sanctuary were located buildings to process the agricultural produce of the estates attached to the monastery and to accommodate artisans involved in industrial processes such as metalworking.

The Anglian kingdom lasted until AD 973 when it was granted to King Kenneth II of Scotland by King Edgar. It was incorporated in the growing Scottish kingdom, which had been created by the unification of the western kingdoms with those of the Picts in the north. Lothian was apparently free of the incursions of the Viking raiders and settlers who brought change to the lands of northern England, northern Scotland and Ireland. The only indication of their presence in Lothian is in the form of 'hogback' gravestones, three of which are known to come from Abercorn. These memorials, named after their characteristic shape, are considered typically Scandinavian in form and are 10th century in date.

Dark Age Sites

The most numerous type of site from this period is the long
cist cemetery, often found accidentally during agricultural or
quarrying activity. These cemeteries have not been included
in the gazetteer, as nothing is visible at the sites and indeed
many of the findspots have been destroyed.

Settlements

1.   * Doon Hill EL
     NT 685 757

Two timber halls and a defensive palisade surrounding the
site have been excavated on the hilltop and the remains are
marked out in concrete. The first hall was a 6th-century
British building; the replacement was a 7th-century Anglian
hall similar to examples from a royal site at Yeavering in
Northumbria. *Historic Scotland.*

Religious sites

2.   * Abercorn WL
     NT 081 791

A monastery (Aebbercurnig) is known to have existed here
by the late 7th century, when Bede reports that Bishop
Trumwine and the monks were driven out by the Picts after
their victory over the Northumbrians at the battle of
Nechtansmere. Parts of two sculptured standing crosses
survive, dated to the 8th century. An oval enclosing bank
only a few centimetres high, visible to the north of the
church, was investigated in 1963 and shown to be a stone-
faced rampart similar to the type found at Iona. Two small
rectangular structures within the bank may have been the
remains of monastic cells. Two complete 10th-century
Scandinavian hogback stones and fragments of a third also
come from this site.

3.   * Aberlady EL
     NT 462 799

Aberlady church has a replica of an 8th-century Anglian

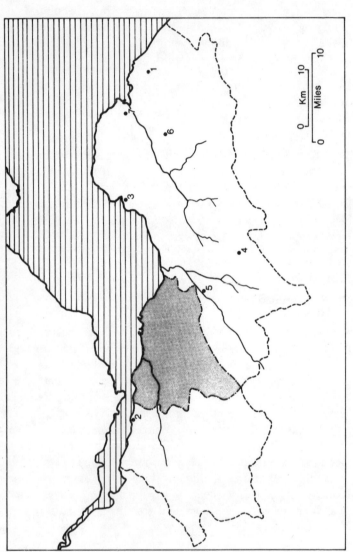

4. Dark Age Sites

cross with the upper part of an angle carved on it. The original is in the collections of the National Museums of Scotland.

4. Borthwick ML
NT 368 596

Fragments of at least three cross-shafts are known. One probably came from the area of the castle in 1886 and was decorated with reliefs of two animals and a key-pattern. The two others are built into the wall of Crookston House (NT 4254 5163) and both are decorated with interlace and borders of cable moulding.

5. Lasswade ML
NT 301 661

Two sculptured stones were found in the ruins of the old parish kirk in the 19th century. One is a side-arm from a standing cross with Christ's arm on the front and a beast on the back; the other shows a four-legged beast in relief.

6. Morham EL
NT 577 726

A fragment of an Anglian cross-slab was found built into the kirkyard wall; it is now in the collections of the National Museums of Scotland.

7. Tyninghame EL
NT 620 797

A monastery, a dependant house of Lindisfarne, was founded at Tyninghame in the 9th century, although no trace is visible. The remains of the 12th-century church survive and may mark the site of the monastery.

THE COUNTRYSIDE
1100 – 1900 AD

The rich and productive land of Lothian has always attracted settlements and until the last 150 years agriculture provided the backbone of the economy of the area. Few traces remain of the medieval agricultural landscape which has suffered the same fate as the medieval towns of the area, destroyed or concealed by changes from the 18th century onwards. Many historic sites are likely to be buried under modern farms. There is enough evidence, however, to show that the normal pattern was of small settlements of tenant farmers and their families in a group of buildings, surrounded by open fields (the infield), cultivated in long strips on the run-rig system, where land was rotated in tenancy. Beyond this area was the outfield, used in common for grazing of animals. The infield was permanently cultivated with cereal crops such as oats and barley, with wheat on good soils, while the outfield was used for grazing, hay and occasionally crops of oats. The best evidence for medieval agriculture is the surviving traces of rig and furrow, formed by the regular ploughing of the same strips of land, pushing up long ridges of earth to make deeper topsoil, and creating furrows to aid drainage. Areas of rig and furrow can often be seen in low, raking sunshine or when light snow accumulates in the furrows. Most can be seen in the upland areas, on the south side of the Lammermuirs and the Pentlands. The earlier centuries of the medieval period were warmer and drier, allowing cultivation of arable crops to high levels. Later worsening of the weather, shrinking populations and a change in the cultivation system of the lower-lying areas made these sites redundant. Remains of some of the farms abandoned over the centuries can still be seen in the hills.

In East Lothian there is good evidence for the existence of medieval villages, similar in their form to those of north-east England, with a village green at their heart and it has been suggested that these villages are the survivors from pre-existing Anglian nucleated settlements. The continuity of

1. The Loth Stone and Traprain Law
(East Lothian)

2. Cairnpapple Henge, Cairn and Stone Circle
(West Lothian)

3. Windmill at Balgone near North Berwick
(East Lothian)

4. Papple Steading near Whittingehame
(East Lothian)

5. The village Tron and Old Parish Church Tower at Stenton
(East Lothian)

6. Temple Preceptory
(West Lothian)

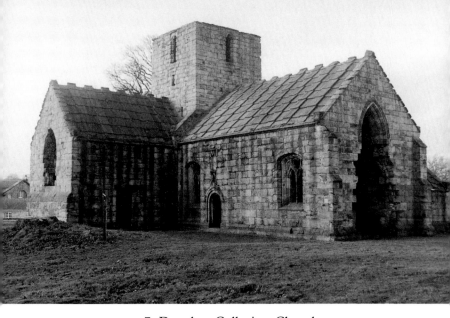

7. Dunglass Collegiate Chapel
(East Lothian)

8. Gifford Parish Kirk
(East Lothian)

9. Seventeenth-century gravestones at Tranent Parish Church
(East Lothian)

10. Linlithgow Palace
(West Lothian)

11. Niddry Castle and shale bing, near Winchburgh
(West Lothian)

12. Borthwick Castle
(Midlothian)

13. Limekilns at Catcraig near Dunbar (East Lothian)

14. Beam pumping engine at Prestongrange
(East Lothian)

15. Hoffman brick-kiln at Prestongrange
(East Lothian)

16. Miner's cottages at Rosewell
(Midlothian)

place-name evidence supports such a theory. Stenton, although extensively rebuilt, gives a clue to the layout of a later medieval village, as records from the 16th century describe its main elements. It had a parish church, main street, a village green, a common loan and a common muir for animals. Houses were ranged along the main street with plots to the rear. Such villages were important social and economic centres for the surrounding countryside. Often the parish church and the laird's house formed the heart of the village. Craftspeople were located in villages, to service the farms of the area. Trade was important and many villages received formal rights to hold markets; some evidence for this survives in the mercat crosses in villages such as Gifford, Preston and Ormiston. A few villages turned themselves into full burghs, with councils and court. These tended to be the flourishing mineral-producing or industrial centres such as Tranent and Prestonpans rather than the small local market centres.

The high lands of the Lammermuirs had been used for cattle grazing, with the farmers living in seasonal structures known as shielings. In the 12th and 13th centuries the monks of Melrose Abbey acquired large tracts of the hills and used them for large numbers of sheep, a valuable commodity in medieval Scotland. The old use of the area survives in names such as Mayshiel, Penshiel and Gamelshiel, while the later monastic ownership is shown in the occurrence of names containing 'grange', the word for a monastic farm, or the prefix 'nun', where the farm belonged to the Cistercian nunnery of Haddington.

The single greatest source of change to agriculture was the 'Improvement' of the 18th century, the product of the Agricultural Revolution. The old system of infield and outfield was swept away over the course of half-a-century and replaced by an enclosed landscape, with small fields surrounded by hedges and stone dykes. Far more land was brought under the plough at lower levels. New crops were introduced, such as peas and beans, to increase soil fertility. Crops were regularly rotated and land was allowed to lie fallow to allow it to recover from overcropping. Liming of fields to neutralise acidity and improve yields was practised on a large scale and a new lime-producing industry sprang up. The old settlements were swept away and replaced by the new model farms, although villages survived. The driving force behind all the changes was, of course, increased profit, and it was the great landowners of East Lothian, such as John Cockburn of Ormiston, Lord Belhaven, the Fletchers of Saltoun and George Rennie of Phantassie, who led the way in Scotland. These developments went hand-in-hand with their attempts to increase the industrial and mineral output of their lands, although there was for some an accompanying desire to improve the conditions and prospects of their tenants.

At the centre of these new farms were built the steadings, many of which survive today, although increasingly converted from agricultural buildings to homes for commuters. Steadings were often built to model patterns and have a degree of consistency in their design. Buildings of stone are arranged around a central courtyard, including cart and granary sheds, byres for animals, stores and a horse mill to house the threshing machine, invented by Andrew Meikle of Saltoun in the 18th century. Sometimes there was a cottage for the tenant. In the earlier examples only three sides of the yard may have had buildings, which are generally single-storey, rubble-built with red pantile roofs.

Increasing prosperity in the 19th century saw many steadings rebuilt in grander architectural style, with symmetrical facades, a central two-storey gateway, doocot and weather vane. The parts of the buildings visible to passers-by often had slate roofs. A typical landmark of these steadings is the tall brick chimney, built over the steam-driven threshing machine, a great advance in agricultural efficiency. At the same time the prosperous tenant farmers built grander houses, removed from the dirty area around the farm buildings, often to a standard box-shaped design with a central staircase. The conditions of the farm workers (many of whom were the smaller tenants dispossessed by the enclosures) improved too. The typical medieval rural dwelling, even for the tenant farmers themselves, had been a long, single-storey house, often built of clay, with a low roof (cruck frame) of turf or thatch. Animals were often accommodated at one end of the house. Seasonal labourers lived in even worse conditions in communal bothies. The Improvement of the 18th century brought investment in new houses for the farm workers, with the construction of stone cottages with tiled roofs, although the practice of accommodating workers in bothies continued to the 20th century.

Some of the most enduring monuments of the agricultural areas are the grain mills which served these farming communities. Water power was abundant and the remains of many mills can still be seen along the length of the rivers of Lothian. These mills were owned on a monopoly basis by landowners who compelled tenants to use them. The mills were built using the landowner's capital and the operation was leased to a miller who charged the tenants for milling their grain, usually around five per cent of its value. The early mills were simple buildings and contained uncomplicated machinery but the changes of the 18th century brought improvements in mill technology, increasing commercialisation and an increase in the scale of operations. In some areas windmills were used on a limited basis, particularly in the coastal areas of East Lothian where rainfall is low.

Some villages which had early origins no longer exist in their original locations. The fashion for parkland settings around large houses in the 18th century saw the demolition of whole villages and the relocation of the inhabitants in new model villages. The earliest of these was Ormiston, soon followed by Gifford (replacing Bothans) and Tyninghame. Often these new villages were encouraged by the landowners to become centres of small local industry, with varying degrees of success. At Athelstaneford the existing settlement was expanded by Sir David Hamilton of Kinloch in the mid-18th century. It was left to the inhabitants to provide the initiative, building new houses and starting new businesses, but the village prospered. By 1778 there were 71 houses and 300 inhabitants and fourteen years later 90 houses and 400 inhabitants. A diversity of trades and industries was carried out, including weaving, brewing, smithing, candlemaking, baking and malting. A meat market was established and the small village smiddy became an agricultural implement works.

Other villages have disappeared almost completely. The reasons are varied. Villages such as Auldcathie (WL) and Morham (EL) fell victim to the gradual decline in the rural population, with little evidence of their past existence apart from their surviving parish churches. Some have left more traces of their existence. At Markle (EL) written records show the existence of a church and 16 houses and crofts each side of a street in the late 16th century. The remains of these can be seen as earthworks along with the remains of the laird's house in an enclosure. The decline of local industries saw the demise of other villages such as St Clements Wells near Falside in East Lothian, where the 19th-century village of 145 inhabitants who were engaged in mining and working at a local distillery now consists only of a farm. As a balance to these losses, the 19th century saw the establishment of whole new communities around the coalfields of Midlothian. The process of change still continues today. Increasing mechanisation of farms has led to a reduction in the number of farm labourers and the character of the rural population has changed dramatically since 1945.

Agricultural Sites

Many hundreds of buildings and structures from the rural history of Lothian still survive, although few are demonstrably medieval in date. The following is a list of some of the best examples of each type, all worth a visit.

Mills

1. **Dunbar EL**
    NT 665 780
West Barns.

2. **East Linton EL**
    NT 594 778
Preston Mill is a fine example of a restored 17th-century mill. It is a single-storey building with an attic and has a circular drying kiln under its red pantile roof, a pond and a lade. A

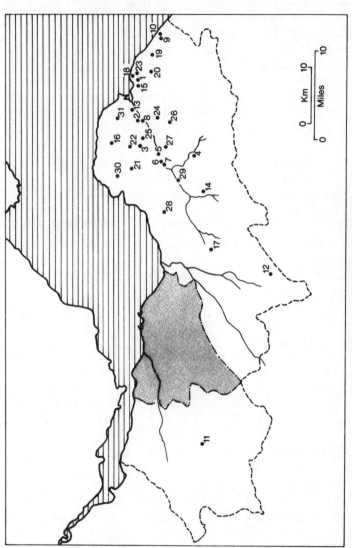

5. The Countryside

separate building holds an office and granary. Demonstrations of the undershot wheel are held when water levels allow. The mill is owned by the National Trust for Scotland who are also responsible for the fine Phantassie doocot, a short walk away, which is of beehive type with 544 nest boxes.

3. East Linton EL
   NT 551 754

Sandy's Mill, upstream from East Linton, is an 18th-century mill which produced pearl barley for grocers and bruised corn for feed.

4. Gifford EL
   NT 532 682

A two-storey sawmill, in Station Road, which served the Gifford estate.

5. Haddington, Abbey Mill EL
   NT 534 747

On the site of the old Cistercian Nunnery mill, the later mill was used for corn.

6. Haddington, Gimmers Mill EL
   NT 519 740

The 14th-century mill, which belonged to the Cistercian nunnery of Haddington, survives as a series of low rubble-built buildings with pantile roofs within the later complex. The mill was greatly extended in the 19th century and is now called Bermaline Mill.

7. Haddington, Poldrate Mill EL
   NT 517 736

The 18th-century three-storey mill and four-storey granary have been restored as a community centre, and the 19th-century iron wheel has been replaced on the wall, albeit as a static feature, but still fed with water from the lade which can be followed for a considerable distance. The mill is on the site of the medieval Kirk Mill, but nothing is immediately identifiable as being of this date. A range of workers' housing can be seen at the rear.

8.   Houston EL
   NT 593 777

A sawmill, once the home of Andrew Meikle, inventor of the mechanised threshing machine, whose grave is in the graveyard opposite.

9.   Innerwick Crowhill EL
   NT 735 741

The remains of a wheelhouse threshing mill are visible north of Innerwick Castle on the Thornton Burn.

10. Innerwick Thornton EL
   NT 741 741

A three-storey mill, originally a monastic mill, on the Thornton Burn approximately 500 yards E of Crowhill.

11. Livingston Mill WL
   NT 033 668

The mill of 1773 on the River Almond in Livingston village has been restored.

12. Newbattle ML
   NT 326 648

A three-storey mill of 1795.

13. Tyninghame EL
   NT 611 790

A sawmill built as part of the model 19th-century estate around Tyninghame House.

14. West Saltoun EL
   NT 469 667

A three-storey corn mill with drying kiln.

Windmills

15. Bielside EL
   NT 654 783

A two-storey tower built of rubble with an external stair, to the rear of Bielside House.

16. Balgone EL
    NT 553 828
The remains of a late 17th-century vaulted tower mill.

17. Cranston ML
    NT 372 651

18. Knockenhair EL
    NT 670 788
The stump of a tower mill.

19. Meikle Pinkerton EL
    NT 703 757
A possible windmill, reused as a doocot.

Steadings

There are very large numbers of post-Improvement farms and steadings in Lothian and more than 135 are recorded in East Lothian alone, where perhaps the best examples are to be found. The following is a subjective list of the 'best' based on a combination of factors, including their architecture and the diversity of their buildings.

20. Doon EL NT 678 760
21. Drem EL NT 510 795
22. East Fortune EL NT 547 793
23. Hallhill, Dunbar EL NT 674 778
24. Luggate, Whittingehame EL NT 595 746
25. Markle Mains EL NT 563 774
26. Papple, Whittingehame EL NT 591 725
27. West Bearford, Haddington EL NT 546 732
28. Greendykes EL NT 436 736
29. Harelaw EL NT 492 708
30. West Fenton EL NT 498 818

Steadings with exceptional facades are *Greendykes* (Classical),

Papple (Gothic), *Phantassie* (Gothic), *Queenstonbank* (Classical), *Sunnyside* (Gothic) and *Traprain* (Gothic). Three are unique: *Eastfield* with Elizabethan-style chimneys, *Spott House* with stables in the Romantic Victorian style and *Hedderwick Hall* built in the neo-Renaissance style.

Teind barn

31. Whitekirk EL
NT 596 816

A fine stone barn built from the stone of the demolished Pilgrim's Hostel, three storeys high, with an external stair to the first floor. The barn was used to store the tithe collected by the church each year. The W end of the building is the remains of a tower-house of 16th-century date.

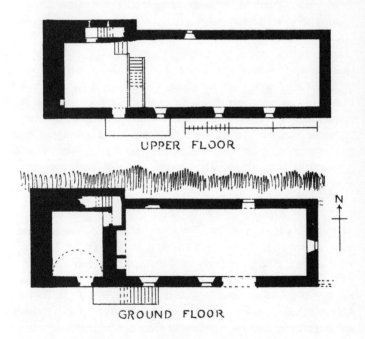

Site Plan 1.
St Mary's, Whitekirk. Plans of the Tithe Barn (**31**)

THE TOWNS OF LOTHIAN
1100 – 1600 AD

The reign of David I between 1124 and 1153 saw many changes to the government, religious life and economy of Scotland. The area where all these changes came together was in the creation of the legal entities known as 'burghs', the towns which have formed the core of society and life in Lothian since the 12th century. These burghs were either 'Royal' if established by the King, or 'burghs of barony' where they were established by the nobility or Church. They had legal rights over their own administration, with councils and courts and rights over trade. The towns were the economic centres for their region as markets and were places where specialised crafts and industries were located.

In other parts of Europe there had been continuous occupation of ancient towns after the collapse of the Roman Empire but in Scotland there was no such tradition. The closest equivalents to towns which may have existed were the great hillfort centres of the Votadini, but these had distinctly different functions, not based on trade and in any case had been out of use for many centuries. The origins of the settlements and economic centres which were granted burgh status are unclear. It has been suggested that it is significant that many of the earliest burghs such as Stirling and Edinburgh, are physically situated on hills and may have grown from pre-existing local strongholds.

The grant of burgh status gave a town inherent advantages over other local settlements, with the monopoly right to overseas trade in the area. In Lothian the dominant burgh was, of course, Edinburgh, and it exploited its position, jealously guarding its rights and drawing increasing amounts of the country's trade through its port at Leith. Nevertheless other burghs were established in Lothian, either as part of David's initiative or as later developments in response to later circumstances and by developing local specialised markets or functions. All the medieval burghs of Lothian were very closely linked to the agricultural land which surrounded them and town and country were closely linked.

While each individual medieval town was different in its details, each had common elements of development. At the heart of the town was its market place, usually a large open space in the early days; this often survives today in a smaller form as the High Street. Around this were laid out plots of lands ('tenements' or 'burgage plots') which were long thin strips of land with a narrow frontage along the market place or street frontage. These seem to have been laid out on a systematic fashion in the early development of the town as many have identical widths and lengths, showing a central authority at work. The early houses were placed at the head of the plot, with gardens behind, where industries and crafts were often located. Gradually, if the town were successful, these plots would become subdivided, with further properties added in the open areas to the rear of the frontage. Access would be made to these plots by the creation of narrow lanes, known as 'closes' along the edge of the plot. In time, further streets might be developed off the main market-place, with the same principles of land division being followed.

The historic burghs of Lothian still display this medieval land division in their modern property boundaries. Haddington, the oldest burgh outside Edinburgh, still has many of its original property boundaries in existence, with the many of the backlands unoccupied, although some closes were opened up to allow sub-division. Dunbar and Linlithgow have the same herringbone pattern of development. Other towns, such as Dalkeith and Bathgate, retain their medieval street pattern, although little else remains of their earlier historic fabric.

Other common elements within medieval towns were the parish kirks, which were often only one of several religious establishments in towns. Most of the monastic orders of medieval Europe, with the exception of the Cistercians, based themselves in towns. Access to a harbour was essential for a burgh, to exercise its rights to foreign trade. Haddington was poorly placed in that respect and used Aberlady as its harbour. It is difficult now to believe that the narrow creek north of Aberlady had ships of 60–70 tons berthing, beached at low tide on the sandbanks. Dunbar had its own harbour, first at Belhaven and then beneath the castle. It gained particular significance as a harbour after the loss of Berwick to the English, being the first major Scottish harbour up the east coast. It was also an important fishing harbour for many centuries and the centre of the herring industry. Few Scottish medieval towns had walls and those defences which did exist were of no great strength as the fragmentary remains of walls at Haddington and Dunbar show.

The history of the development of medieval towns of Lothian outside Edinburgh is not particularly well document-ed and there has been little urban archaeology which could cast light on the types and quantity of crafts and industries carried out in them. We know from the historical records that Scotland's main trade overseas was in raw materials, with the export of large quantities of wool and hides, with finished goods being brought in as imports. The implications for the towns are clear, with such trading patterns suggesting that local industries were small-scale and localised. The main function of towns in Lothian was as market centres for the surrounding countryside to which they were closely linked, and on the productivity of which they depended to a large degree. The other side of the monopoly of overseas trade which the burghs held was of course that the towns suffered when trade was disrupted, as it was in the 13th century by the Wars of Independence with England and in the 14th century by the shrinking populations of Europe after the Black Death. It is generally believed that most Scottish burghs suffered serious decline until 1500. It is a little difficult in this context to understand the scale of expenditure on the magnificent burgh kirks which were built in Linlithgow and Haddington during the 15th century and they could be seen as defiance in the face of economic adversity.

Lothian suffered badly during the invasions by the English of the 1540s and a description of Haddington by Daniel Defoe in the early 18th century shows that much of the damage there was never repaired by his time. In contrast to the supposed problems of the larger towns in the later medieval period, the rural areas had seen an increasing number of smaller settlements becoming burghs of barony, mainly to allow them to hold local markets, presumably at the expense of the established market centres. Indeed the smaller settlements in East Lothian grew in prosperity during the 16th and 17th centuries and most had the right to hold markets by the end of the 17th century. New, fully fledged towns grew from the mining and industrial centres of Tranent (1542), Prestonpans (1552) and Cockenzie (1591) and they exercised all their rights to election of councils and courts as a result of their growing wealth and importance.

The wealth created by the agricultural improvements, mining and industrialisation of the 18th and 19th centuries saw the transformation of many of the towns of Lothian, with the demolition of many of the older buildings and the creation of fine commercial and public buildings, symbols of local entrepreneurship and pride. Haddington regained its importance as the major grain market in one of the richest agricultural areas of the country and was almost completely rebuilt, many of the buildings surviving today as a reminder of its prosperity. New centres became important, populations grew and shifted from the land to the new industries, a process that continued into the 19th century. The new town of Livingston, established in 1962, is simply the latest in a line of descent which began in the 12th century. The economic success of this new settlement, with new, alien architectural ideas, based on a new planned layout decided by a central authority, attracting industry and economic growth to previously rural areas, is a fine symbol of the impact David's burghs must have had on pre-urban Scotland.

Burghs

Too little space is available within this volume to describe all of the burghs of Lothian, so a representative selection has been chosen.

Aberlady EL

Now a small dormitory village, it had considerable importance during the medieval period as the port of

Haddington. It later gained importance as a local market and as a centre of weaving. The medieval High Street, with the stump of the Mercat Cross, remains the axis of the village. The harbour was in the creek to the north, with Sea Wynd, now the main road, giving access. A rubble-built warehouse at the corner of the two roads is a reminder of the mercantile past. The parish church is still in use; the remains of Luffness Priory lie to the E of the village.

Bathgate WL

Little survives of the medieval burgh except the street names and the ruined old parish kirk. It was a medieval market and administrative centre, much changed and expanded by the discovery of oil-shale nearby in the 19th century.

Dalkeith ML

Dalkeith was a burgh of barony, established by the Douglas family and later, as so much of the area, under the feudal sway of the Buccleuchs. The High Street was the medieval market-place and the parish church survives, now known as East Church. Dalkeith House contains the remains of the medieval castle. The Old Tolbooth dates from the 17th century.

Dunbar EL

An early burgh of barony, it became a royal burgh in 1445, partially in recognition of its strategic importance following the loss of Berwick to the English. Excavations at the NW end of the High Street in Castlepark have shown Dunbar to have its origins in an important Anglian settlement, with the discovery of the remains of timber halls and a fragment of a bishop's gold cross. The High Street was the market area and survives to its full width, with the plan of the medieval burgage plots preserved in the closes either side. The lower part of the Mercat Cross has been moved and now is outside the Tolbooth, which is of 17th-century origin. The remains of the castle overlook the harbour, which was an important regional centre for fishing. The harbour is in fact three separate constructions; the Old Harbour, built in 1574 and

1650, Broad Haven and the Victoria Harbour of 1844. A fragment of the late medieval town wall can be seen in Bamburgh's Close north of the High Street. The parish church is 19th century, but the church tower of the Trinitarian Priory survives in Friarscroft outside the old town limits.

Haddington EL

The town retains its medieval form, with a very large triangular market place formed by High Street and Market Street, closed off on the short side by Sidegate. The Mercat Cross in the High Street is a 19th-century replacement of a medieval original. The Custom Stone, the place where the customs dues were paid, can be seen in Sidegate. The centre of the market triangle is filled by an island of buildings, a process begun in the 15th/16th centuries and completed in the 17th and 18th. The lines of the medieval burgage plots survive intact in many places behind the fine buildings of the 18th and 19th centuries. A good example of a subdivided burgage plot can be seen at Mitchell's Close off Market Street. A short section of the town wall survives at NT 515 742. The church of St Mary is the largest medieval parish church in Scotland and is sited picturesquely next to the river. The importance of Haddington as a milling centre on the Tyne is shown by the Poldrate and Gimmers Mills at ends of Sidegate.

Linlithgow WL

A royal burgh of David I, the town is dominated by the remains of the royal palace and the massive 15th-century burgh kirk. Little else survives to show the importance of the town in the medieval period, although 17th-century houses can be seen at 40–42 and 44–48 High Street and West Port House.

Musselburgh EL

Founded as a burgh of barony by the Abbey of Dunfermline sometime between 1315 and 1328, Musselburgh lies at the crossing of the Esk and had a harbour in the estuary. The shellfish beds of the Forth were an important resource. Fisherrow was a replacement harbour built in the 16th century when the estuary silted up. A wide High Street contains the fine Tolbooth of 1590. The river was crossed in the 16th century, or even earlier, by the Old Roman Bridge. Pinkie House was the 16th-century home of the Abbot of Dunfermline and its tower now lies at the heart of Loretto School.

North Berwick EL
Created a burgh of barony of the Earl of Douglas in 1373, the town later became a royal burgh. Its main significance was as an embarkation point for the pilgrims heading to St Andrews. The medieval parish church and the Cistercian nunnery survive as partial ruins. North Berwick became a holiday centre with the arrival of the branch railway in the 19th century.

Prestonpans EL
The burgh had its origins in the 12th-century harbour of Aldhamer, granted to the monks of Newbattle Abbey. The coastal zone down to Cockenzie was an important mining, industrial and fishing centre until recent times. Along with Preston, now reduced in size and importance, it was made a burgh of barony in 1552 as an important market centre. The only historic building of note still standing in Prestonpans is the tower of the late 16th-century church, while Preston is more fortunate, with its mercat cross, tower and two fine 17th-century mansions (Hamilton and Northfield Houses).

Tranent EL
A centre of mining from the 13th century onwards, it was created a burgh of barony in 1541–2. Little remains of the historic town except the kirkyard with its fine 18th-century gravestones and the ruin of the late 16th-century tower nearby.

CHURCHES AND RELIGIOUS HOUSES
1100 – 1900 AD

As described earlier, Christianity most probably came to Lothian in the 5th and 6th centuries, but there are few traces of the earliest places of worship, only a hint of the monastery at Abercorn and fragments of some Early Christian stone crosses. The earliest evidence for church buildings in Lothian belongs to the early part of the 12th century but the continuous use of many of the medieval churches of Lothian to the present day has resulted in the destruction of many of their original features by later alterations. The best visible evidence often survives in the churches which were abandoned when new churches were built in the centuries after the Reformation, although with careful observation medieval features and plans can be discerned in other churches. Within the gazetteer only those churches which have surviving medieval evidence are listed. There are many other sites where only the burying ground survives but no building, or which are known only from an imprecise reference; most of these have not been included.

The large number of medieval churches which do survive are the direct result of the policies and actions of King David I, who had strong links with the great Norman royal families of Northern Europe. These rulers presided over a blossoming of culture, art and religion across their realms in the late 11th and 12th centuries. David is generally believed to have introduced the parish system to Scotland, each small geographical area having its own church and priest. This is still the administrative basis for the all the major Christian denominations.

Of these early churches, many of which were highly decorated, the best example is that at Tyninghame, which survives now only as a strange skeleton of decorated stonework. It was simply a long, thin rectangular church with an apse and a chancel, separated by an arch from the nave with a tower at the west end, all decorated in the Romanesque style. Fragments of plainer decorative work of this period survive at Uphall and Abercorn. The remains of churches of the later 12th and 13th centuries are less common. In this period it has been observed, however, by architectural historians that the form of the church changes to a simple rectangular box shape, with no arch between the nave and chancel and this shape remains common through the rest of the medieval period.

The next major episode of church building in Scotland was the 15th century, with the construction of many 'collegiate' churches. For many years it had been the custom of wealthy patrons to pay for the dedication of chantry chapels within parish kirks, where a priest prayed for the benefactor and his family. In the 15th century these were superseded by churches with colleges of priests attached. Often the local parish church was simply taken over and demolished completely to allow the establishment of the new college. Despite the wealth of the patrons many of these churches, such as the best known, Roslin, were never finished, or, like Seton, were finally completed by the descendants of the founder. From this same period of church building come the two great burgh kirks of Lothian – Haddington and Linlithgow, symbols of the civic pride of the inhabitants.

As well as the introduction of the parish system, David I was responsible for encouraging the establishment of monasteries and abbeys in Scotland by the religious orders of Europe, and he was responsible for the foundation of many of them. It is known that most of the major orders were present in Lothian, but the remains of most of their buildings were demolished after the Reformation of 1560–61. The monasteries, abbeys and priories of these orders were laid out to a common plan, although individual orders had their own variations. The plan can be seen in a modern form at Nunraw Abbey in the foothills of the Lammermuirs above Garvald. It had an open garden space at the heart, surrounded by a covered walkway, forming the cloister, with the other buildings of the members of the order ranged on all four sides – the church, the sleeping quarters (dorter), the eating area (the refectory), stores and the chapter house, where the monks met to administer the establishment collectively under the abbot or prior. Outside the main cloister ranges were the guest-house, the hospital and the agricultural buildings, for the religious houses were often the centres of large estates. They also possessed large landholdings throughout the county, mostly let to tenants. One small grange (a monastic farm run directly by the Mother-House) has survived well at Moorfoot. Abbeys elsewhere also had rights in the rich agricultural lands of Lothian, such as Melrose Abbey which held large possessions in the Lammermuirs, mainly for sheep-farming. The monasteries also had rights over mineral exploitation, given by patrons. For example, Newbattle Abbey was mining coal in Lothian in the 13th century and had rights over salt production at Prestonpans.

Newbattle was the only great abbey in Lothian outside Edinburgh and was a Cistercian house founded in 1140. The Cistercians preferred rural locations for their abbeys, in the pursuit of spiritual peace. Other Cistercian houses were nunneries at North Berwick – fragmentary remains of which survive – Haddington and also Manuel a Nun's house near Linlithgow. The remains of the other orders are very slight such as part of the church of the Carmelite friary at Luffness and the church of the Knight's Hospitallers at Torphichen. Excavations at the site of the Whitefriars at Linlithgow have shown that remains of these buildings can survive under the ground. Excavation of the hospital at Soutra on its exposed hilltop have recently produced interesting evidence for the practice of medicine in the medieval period. One very important aspect of medieval religious life was the pilgrimage, the long journey to places associated with saints and Lothian was on the route of one of the main pilgrimages of medieval Europe, to St Andrews, via Whitekirk, the site of a holy well and North Berwick.

The religious houses suffered badly after the Reformation of 1560, with the loss of their landholdings and the privatisation of their buildings. While the effect of this was not overnight, the remains were gradually demolished, with only Newbattle being incorporated into a new house on the site. The parish churches of Lothian mostly continued in use; the liturgy changed to the Protestant rites and the internal arrangements of the churches changed, with the focus of the church shifting from the east end to the pulpit halfway along the wall of the church. Gradually churches were rebuilt, often, from the early 18th century, on a T-plan, with the pulpit along the long wall and an aisle facing it, often for the local laird and his family. The 19th century saw the Gothic revival and the heavy-handed attempts of many architects to recreate what they felt to be 'authentic' medieval architecture. The unfortunate side-effect of much of this was the destruction of surviving medieval features. The 19th century also saw the proliferation of smaller sects and breakaway denominations; description of their history and buildings is beyond the scope of this volume.

Medieval religious houses

All sites where the existence of a religious house is definitely known are included in this section, although at some nothing remains above ground level.

1.   * Dunbar Red Friars EL
     NT 678 788

A Trinitarian priory founded in 1218 by the 5th Earl of Dunbar, subsequently refounded 1240–1248. Dissolved in 1529 it was a small establishment with only the 15th-century tower surviving today, converted into a doocot. Excavations have located the remains of the church, with parts of a glazed tile floor still in place.

2.   Fidra EL
     NT 512 868

Ruin of the chapel of St Nicholas, a religious house served by canons from Dryburgh Abbey, recorded as existing prior to 1220. The rectangular nave and chancel are visible as foundations but only the N wall survives to any height. A graveyard lies outside.

3.   Haddington, Greyfriars EL
     NT 518 739

This Franciscan Friary was founded in 1242, destroyed by

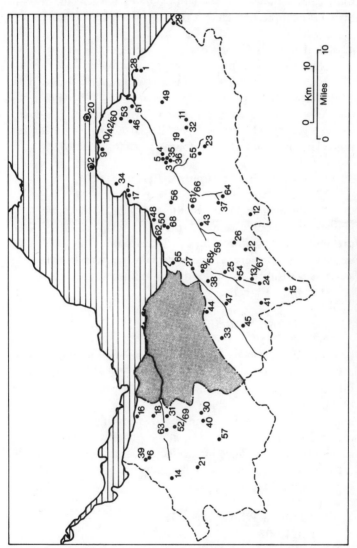

6. Churches and Religious Houses

the English 1356, and then rebuilt. It was originally known as
the 'Lamp of Lothian' until destroyed by the English. No
trace remains above ground but part of the site in Church
Street is occupied by Holy Trinity Episcopalian Church.

4. Haddington Priory EL
NT 533 746 (approx)

Cistercian nunnery of the Blessed Virgin Mary founded in
1159 whose site is uncertain but seems to have been close to
the Abbey Bridge over the River Tyne, east of the town
where a graveyard survives SE of the farm. One of the largest
nunneries in Scotland, the site was secularised in 1621.

5. * Haddington, St Martin's EL
NT 521 739

On Whittingehame Drive on the east side of the town, it is
known as a possession of the Cistercian nunnery (see
previous entry) in the late 12th century. Only the nave
survives, well preserved, and is a plain box with buttresses a
secondary feature to support the tunnel vault which was
added in the 13th century.

6. Linlithgow, Whitefriars WL
NT 003 765

Excavations in 1984 uncovered the remains of the church,
the E range and some of the S range of the Carmelite Friary
founded in 1401. The friars took over a pre-existing chapel
of the 13th century which they extended to the E with a
chancel. The E range contained the sacristy, a chapter-house
and a parlour, with the dormitory possibly above. The S
range seems to have been the refectory. Burials were found in
the church, cloister area and in a graveyard to the N and E of
the excavated ranges.

7. * Luffness, Whitefriars EL
NT 471 802

A Carmelite friary, existing by 1293, which is now an
atmospheric ruin easily accessible within the woodland
around Luffness House. The remains of a simple church,

27m by 6m, are visible although only the lowest courses of the walls survive. Among the monuments are a 13th-century knight's effigy and the tomb slab in the floor of Kentigern Hepburn, dating to *c.* 1500. Nothing else of the friary survives above ground.

8. * Newbattle Abbey ML
NT 333 361

A Cistercian house of the Blessed Virgin Mary, founded 1140 as a Daughter-House of Melrose. From 1580 onwards part of the abbey was converted into a house which survives at the core of the current building. The house incorporates part of the S end of the monastic range, with the dorter undercroft intact, dating to the 14th/15th century. The main abbey remains lie buried to the W and N of the original house, with the church situated to the N of the extension built in 1968. The remains of the abbey church, which was 94m long, with a nave, chancel and transepts, are exposed in the grass.

9. * North Berwick Priory EL
NT 546 850

A Cistercian nunnery founded *c.* 1150 and secularised in 1588. Now the site of a nursing home in Old Abbey Road, all that survives above ground are the remains of a late medieval range running E-W, probably forming the N range of the claustral buildings with the cloister area therefore lying to the south in the garden, with the church beyond on the S side of that.

10. North Berwick EL
NT 558 856

A hospital for the poor and pilgrims, founded by Duncan, 4th Earl of Fife in 1154, probably stood on the site occupied by the granaries on the E side of the road near the harbour.

11. * Nunraw Abbey EL
NT 593 700

The Cistercian Abbey of Sancta Maria, founded in 1946,

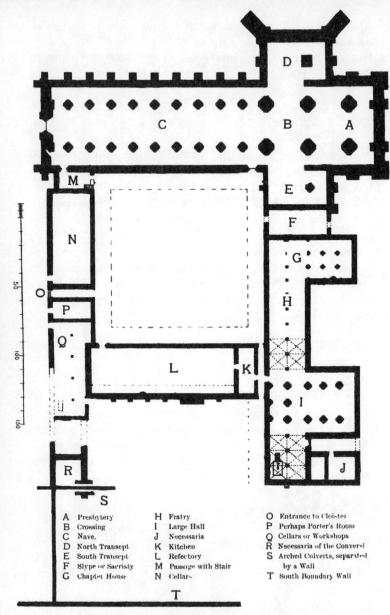

Site Plan 2.
Newbattle Abbey. Plan (**8**)

A	Presbytery	H	Fratry	O	Entrance to Cloister.
B	Crossing	I	Large Hall	P	Perhaps Porter's Room
C	Nave.	J	Necessaria	Q	Cellars or Workshops
D	North Transept	K	Kitchen	R	Necessaria of the Conversi
E	South Transept	L	Refectory	S	Arched Culverts, separated
F	Slype or Sacristy	M	Passage with Stair		by a Wall
G	Chapter House	N	Cellars	T	South Boundary Wall

adjacent to the road between Garvald and Duns is a modern version of the medieval cloister and associated ranges, thereby giving a fine impression of the appearance of the lost monastic buildings of Lothian. The cloister ranges were built between 1953 and 1969.

12. Soutra Hospital ML
NT 423 584

All that remains of the large medieval hospital of the Holy Trinity on the hilltop is the burial aisle of the Pringles of Soutra which in fact considerably post-dates the years of operation of the hospital which was founded in c. 1164 by Malcolm IV for the welfare of travellers. Excavations in recent years have uncovered some of the buildings of the hospital and evidence for medical practice has been found. The aisle itself is 8m long with a stone roof. The date over the doorway is 1686.

13. * Temple Preceptory ML
NT 315 387

Close to the B6372, the Preceptory of the Knights Templar was founded in 1175 and passed to the Knights of St John in 1312 following the suppression of the Templars. The church later became the parish church and was finally abandoned in 1832. The roofless ruin visible today seems to be 14th-century in date, but on the site of an earlier church. The W end is post-Reformation.

14. * Torphichen Preceptory WL
NS 969 725

The only establishment within Scotland of the Knights of St John of Jerusalem. The preceptory was founded by 1153 and surrendered to the Crown in 1560. Of the cruciform church, partially 12th-century, but much altered in the 14th/15th centuries, only the tower and transepts survive, with the site of the nave occupied by the new parish church built in 1756. This is still decorated and maintained as the priory Church of the Order of St John in Scotland. To the north are the remains of the domestic ranges and cloister of the preceptory.

Associated with the preceptory are several stones, reputed to mark the boundaries of the sanctuary area around the church. These survive at NS 9806 7311, NS 9563 7078, both of which had crosses of St John carved on their faces (now disappeared); at NS 9909 7270 which has been moved and built into a dyke 500m N of Lower Craigmailen, but still has fine decoration of patriarchial crosses on both faces; and also at NS 968 725. Another stone stands within the kirkyard at NS 9864 7250. *Historic Scotland.*

15. Moorfoot ML
NT 296 523

The remains of a monastic grange are visible in the form of footings forming a courtyard 30m square, with a range of three rooms on the south side which were probably domestic and another range on the N, with a substantial square structure on the NW corner, possibly a gatehouse. The E side has been eroded by the burn. To the N an L-shaped earthwork may be a floodbank.

Parish and collegiate churches

16. Abercorn WL
NT 0814 7910

The blocked S door is the only surviving architectural detail of the 12th-century parish church which was reconstructed in 1579 and 1893. The church was originally a simple rectangular form with nave and chancel. Subsequent to the reconstruction in 1579, the Philpstoun enclosure (1727) and the Binns aisle (1618) were added to the S side of the nave, and the Duddingston aisle (1603) to the chancel (which was itself later converted to the Hopetoun aisle in 1708). The N aisle was built in the works of 1893, when *ersatz* Norman-style detailing was to added to the chancel arch and the W end. The graveyard contains a good collection of post-Reformation carved gravestones.

17. Aberlady EL
NT 462 798
The 15th-century rubble-built tower is all that survives of the medieval church, at the W end of the building of 1886.

18. Auldcathie WL
NT 079 760
The ruin of a simple single-chambered rectangular, pre-Reformation church of which only the gable ends survive well. Some 14th-century architectural fragments incorporated in the structure show it to have been rebuilt. A graveyard surrounds the church. The village which the church served has disappeared.

19. Baro EL
NT 557 705
Nothing survives of the old parish church except the burial ground.

20. Bass Rock Chapel EL
NT 604 872
The ruin of the castle chapel survives as a small rectangular building to the N of the castle site. It had windows in the W and S walls and a door in the S. Inside are a piscina and a stoup by the door.

21. Bathgate Old Parish Kirk WL
NS 990 682
The ruins of the single-chambered structure, given by Malcolm IV (1153–65) to Holyrood Abbey, are medieval, although little of the architectural detail survives apart from the N door jambs (c. 1200), a small window and a mid-13th-century effigy of a priest inside.

22. Borthwick ML
NT 369 596
The Norman church of St Mungo was granted by David I to Scone Priory in the mid-12th century. The current church, mainly rebuilt in 1862–4, incorporates a 12th-century apse

and the S chancel wall from the original church, and a 15th-century vestry and S transept with its tunnel-vault roof which is thought to have been built by the first Lord Borthwick who was responsible for the construction of the magnificent castle nearby. The tomb with carved effigies beneath a decorated canopy has been dated to *c.* 1450 and is identified as that of Borthwick and his wife. Some of the original colours of the paint can be seen on the highly detailed representations of the lord and his lady.

23. * Bothans Collegiate Church EL
   NT 546 671

Access to this chapel which lies in the grounds of Yester House is best made along the drive which leads from the village of Gifford and the church lies within the woods. Collegiate church of St Cuthbert, founded 1421 by Sir William Hay and others, originally called Bothans, later Yester. Obviously intended to be cruciform, there is no nave (it was either not built or has been demolished). The blocking wall across the transepts has magnificent Gothic decoration dating to 1753, designed by the Adam brothers. In the interior are 15th-century tunnel vaults; the chancel arch is thought to be dated to 1688.

24. Clerkington ML
   NT 306 576

The remains of the walls, grass-covered, survive 0.7m high, forming a rectangular chapel which lies within a graveyard enclosed by a low turf-covered wall.

25. Cockpen Old Parish Church ML
   NT 327 633

A simple ruin with some carved details of 13th-century date and later burial aisles, including one of the Dalhousie family.

26. Crichton Collegiate Church ML
   NT 381 616

A collegiate church was founded in 1449 by William, Lord Crichton, on the site of a pre-existing church. It consists of a chancel and transepts, all with simple stone vaults, with a tower over the crossing; it is unclear whether the nave was ever built. The galleries inside were fitted in 1729. Restored in 1898, few ancient features survive inside the church.

27. * Dalkeith Collegiate Church (now East Church) ML
NT 333 675

On the W side of High Street, the medieval church of St Nicholas was made collegiate in 1406 and became a parish church in 1467. The college of priests was enlarged by the first Earl of Morton in 1477 and he increased the E end of the church in size soon after. This fine late-Gothic choir, with two bays and a three-sided apse, was walled off from the rest of the church in 1590 and remains as a shell which contains the tomb of Morton and his wife Joanna, although the effigies are badly weathered. The main body of the church was rebuilt in 1851–2 by David Bryce, leaving intact only the arcades and tower arch of *c.* 1400 of the structure of the original medieval church. The Buccleuch family vault is in the former sacristy.

28. Dunbar Collegiate Church EL
NT 682 786

The College of St Bey was founded in 1342, but nothing survives from the medieval building, which was rebuilt in 1819–21, although the decorative monument of George Home, who died in 1611, is preserved in the N aisle.

29. * Dunglass Collegiate Church EL
NT 767 719

The college of St Mary was founded *c.* 1450 by Sir Alexander Home, although there may have been a chapel here by 1423. The present building is from the 15th century and was originally a simple nave and chancel, but the design was changed to cruciform during construction. All the limbs of the church have tunnel-vaults, with stone roof-slabs above. The tower was used defensively during the attacks by the English under the Earl of Hertford in 1544. Later the church was used as a barn with the E wall and window removed for access purposes. *Historic Scotland.*

30. East Calder Old Parish Church WL
   NT 084 678

The ruin of St Cuthbert's kirk, 16th-century in date, is a plain rectangular box which has been disused since 1750 and is now divided into three plain burial enclosures.

31. Ecclesmachan WL
   NT 069 735

Only two early 13th-century doorways survive of the medieval church of St Machan which was changed to the post-Reformation T-plan in 1710.

32. Garvald EL
   NT 580 700

A Norman masonry string course is visible, reused within the considerable rebuilding of 1829. A sundial of 1633 can be seen on the S wall.

33. Glencorse ML
   1. NT 216 639
   2. NT 245 630

1. The remains of the chapel of St Catherine lie under the waters of the reservoir. It was probably in use from the 13th century until 1635.
2. The ruin of the old parish church, dating to 1665, was originally rectangular but was later modified by two family aisles in the late 17th century. A new church was built in 1883.

34. Gullane EL
   NT 481 827

The kirk of St Andrew was abandoned in 1612 and the ruin turned into burial vaults. The surviving medieval details include a Norman chancel arch with decorated column capitals and a late medieval chapel on the N of the nave.

35. Haddington EL

Haddington had many churches and chapels in the medieval period; many of the smaller ones have disappeared and their existence is known only from documentary sources. As well as the religious houses described above, there are records of churches or chapels of St Laurence, St Kentigern, St Ann, St John, St Catherine and a 'chapel on the Fleshmarket'.

36. Haddington St Mary's EL
NT 519 736

Founded as a Norman church in 1139, it was destroyed in 1356 by the English invaders and subsequently rebuilt. It received collegiate status in c. 1540 but was badly damaged by the English during the siege of 1548. The nave was repaired but the rest was unused until 1971 when it was restored. The church is large (longer than St Giles in Edinburgh) almost 63m long and cruciform and more impressive in the scale than the execution. The restored vaulting in the choir and transepts is, remarkably, made of fibreglass. The medieval sacristy was converted into the family aisle for the Lauderdales and contains some fine monuments.

37. Keith EL
NT 449 645

The ruined 13th-century church lies opposite the front of Keith Marischal house. The E wall has two windows of c. 1200, the S a late medieval lancet window. There is a fine decorated memorial of the Anderson family of Whitburn, 1685–95.

38. Lasswade Old Parish Church ML
NT 319 642

The tower, at the W end, is all that remains of the medieval church. Abandoned in 1793, the ruins collapsed in 1866. A 15th-century effigy of a knight survives in the burial aisle of the Prestons; other burial aisles of the Drummonds and the Clerks of Eldin survive. The churchyard contains several 18th-century carved tombstones.

39. Linlithgow, St Michael's WL
   NT 002 773

The parish kirk of St Michael's was built in its current form between 1425 and 1530 after a fire in 1424. One of the masons, John Frenssh (died 1489) is buried in the N nave aisle. Restored in 1812 and 1894–96 it is the second largest church in Lothian, cruciform, with the tower placed at the W end rather than over the crossing. The tower is small in scale compared to the bulk of the church. The spire is aluminium, erected in 1964 as a replacement for the medieval crown steeple which was removed in about 1821. Internally the highlight is the window of the S transept chapel, considered one of the finest pieces of late Gothic medieval tracery carvings in Scotland.

40. Mid Calder WL
   NT 075 675

A T-plan church, the choir was begun before 1542 by the rector Master Peter Sandilands, but the rest of the church as planned, with a nave, porch and steeple, was never built. There is fine window tracery in the S wall but the N wall is plain and examination of the exterior shows that a cloister was to be built, with corbels ready for it, presumably to house a college of priests. The transept was added in 1863.

41. Mount Lothian ML
   NT 275 570

This medieval chapel was originally granted to the monks of Holyrood Abbey in 1240. The walls of the chapel survive 0.3m high. The chancel was probably secondary to the nave. The walled enclosure around the chapel is the graveyard.

42. North Berwick, St Andrew's EL
   NT 554 886

Founded by 1177, it was a ruin by 1656, when it was replaced. Little remains of the former parish kirk except a small vaulted structure which projected from the S wall of the church. The foundations of the north and south aisles, the tower and part of the nave have been exposed.

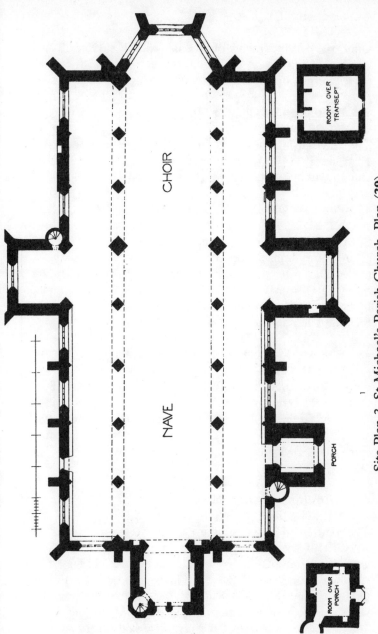

Site Plan 3. St Michael's Parish Church. Plan (**39**)

43. Ormiston EL
NT 411 676

Only part of the remains of St Giles church survives. It is a roofless aisle, with an arch-headed window of 13th-century date; Norman decorated stonework is built into walls nearby.

44. Pentland Old Church ML
NT 262 663

The graveyard of the parish kirk (known to exist from before 1275 until 1647) survives, but the exact location of the church within it is uncertain.

45. Penicuik Old Parish Church ML
NT 237 596

St Mungo's old church is a ruin in the churchyard of the later 18th-century replacement. It consists of the tower and the W gable. The lower part of the tower is late 17th century, the belfry dates from 1731–2. The site of the church is occupied by burials and monuments including the mausoleum built by Sir John Clerk for his wife in 1684.

46. * Preston Kirk, East Linton EL
NT 592 798

The 1770 church of St Baldred (further altered in 1891) contains the remains of a fine 13th-century chancel built in the early Gothic style; the E gable and part of the S wall survive to the wall-head. A holy well, consisting of a small stone-lined cavity is hidden *c.* 50m E of the church (NT 5931 7780).

47. * Roslin Collegiate Chapel
NT 274 630

The buttresses of St Matthew's church are visible in the kirkyard of the Collegiate church which replaced it. This latter (unique) church is the chapel of the college of St Matthew founded in 1450 by William Sinclair, 3rd Earl of Orkney. Only the choir, sacristy and part of the transepts were complete by the time of the death of its founder in 1484. The foundations of the rest were laid but never built upon and are visible in the graveyard. The whole of the structure, inside and out, is covered in amazing elaborate decoration of late-Gothic motifs, including figured sculptures without parallel in Scotland. The most famous element is the 'Prentice Pillar', named after the apocryphal story of the apprentice who carved it being killed by the master mason because of the perfect skill he displayed. Admission restricted.

48. * Seton Collegiate Church EL
NT 418 751

The church of St Mary and the Holy Cross was founded as a college in 1492 by the second Lord Seton on the site of an earlier parish church known to date from at least 1242. The foundations of the nave of this earlier church survive as foundations to the W, leaving the church T-shaped. The choir and sacristy were the work of the first Lord Seton (died 1478) while the second and third Lords added stone vaults and roofing, and the widow of the third (who died at Flodden) added the transepts and tower. A new church was built elsewhere in the 17th century and so this chapel was used for farm buildings. It was restored in 1878. The fine building and picturesque setting make it worth a visit. *Historic Scotland.*

49. Stenton Old Parish Church EL
NT 622 743

The ruin of a plain rectangular 16th-century kirk with a tower at the W end, replaced by the new church in 1829. The Rood Well at the E end of the village (NT 624 744) is a fine medieval holy well inside a circular stone building with conical stone roof.

50. Tranent Old Parish Church EL
NT 403 735

The medieval church was mainly replaced by a new building at the start of the 19th century although small fragments of medieval stonework survive in W and S walls (including a doorway in the S wall) and on the N side is the aisle of the

Cadells which is pre-Reformation.

51. Tyninghame EL
NT 620 797

The possible site of the earlier Dark Age monastery of St
Baldred, this is a fine, ruined 12th-century parish church in
the gardens of Tyninghame House. It was in use until 1761
when the old village was cleared away in estate works. All the
masonry was removed with the exception of the decorated
details and the arches, leaving a skeleton framework. It is a
fine example of a Romanesque church, highly decorated and
of typical Scottish-Norman form, with an oblong nave, a
square chancel with a semicircular apse and a narrow W
tower.

52. Uphall, St Nicholas WL
NT 060 722

A 12th-century parish church with surviving masonry in the
W tower, nave and chancel, with Norman decoration on the
S door of the nave. The chancel was extended in the 13th
century and the church has been much altered since then,
with major episodes of reworking in 1878 and 1937.

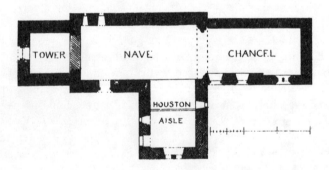

Site Plan 4. Uphall Church. Plan (**52**)

53. Whitekirk EL
NT 596 815

Originally this was a simple 12th-century parish church, dedicated to the Virgin Mary, under the control of Holyrood Abbey. A number of miracles at the holy well nearby (*c.* NT 5981 8166) attracted large numbers of pilgrims and the church was placed under the King's protection. Hostels were built close to the church by James I *c.* 1430 to house the pilgrims. These were demolished *c.* 1540 and the stones were used to build Sinclair's Tower which forms part of the Tithe Barn 100m N of the church. The church was badly damaged internally by fire set by suffragettes in 1914. All that remains of the medieval complex is a simple cruciform church, with a plain interior.

Post-Reformation churches : 1500 – 1900 AD

Many of the churches listed above continued in use after the Reformation with only the internal arrangements changed. Few completely new churches were built until the 19th century; these are listed below.

54. Carrington ML
NT 318 605

A T-plan kirk with projecting tower, in the same form as Gifford, with which it shares a construction date of 1710. It replaced the old parish church to the NE which is the site of the 18th-century Ramsay mausoleum.

55. Gifford EL
NT 534 681

The T-plan kirk with a tower projecting from the W wall was built in 1710 as part of the new model village built to replace the medieval village of Bothans which lay around the old church which still stands (p. 86, **23** above). The kirk has a 17th-century Dutch-style decorated pulpit.

56. Gladsmuir Old Parish Church EL
NT 450 730

The old church is the ruin of an elongated building of 1695, with a fine bellcote at the W end. It stands behind the new church built in 1838.

57. Livingston Village WL
NT 036 638

A simple rectangular rebuild of 1732 on old footings with a bellcote at the W end.

58. Newbattle ML
NT 331 661

A T-plan kirk of 1727 with a projecting tower on the fourth side, similar to Carrington and Gifford.

59. Newton ML
NT 334 690

A T-plan kirk of 1742. The remains of the 17th-century tower of the earlier Old Church stand *c.* 1km S of Newton House, owing their survival to their incorporation as a picturesque feature in the designed landscape around Dalkeith Palace.

60. North Berwick Old Parish Church EL
NT 553 852

The plain rectangular shell of the church survives with a tower at the W end. The church dates from 1659 onwards and was used until 1861. There seem to have been two phases of construction, the second in the late 18th century.

61. Pencaitland EL
NT 443 690

A late 16th/early 17th-century chapel, built on a rectangular plan with a single chamber with a tower at the W end (dated 1631). The chapel on the N side survives from the medieval period. A striking memorial in the church to Kathleen Forbes shows East Lothian's trading links with Holland.

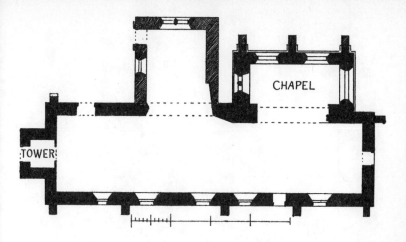

Site Plan 5. Pencaitland Church. Plan (**61**)

62. Prestonpans EL
NT 387 747

The earliest post-Reformation chapel in Lothian, built in 1596, of which only the tower and S door survive; the rest was much altered in a rebuilding of 1774.

Post-Reformation gravestones

Good groups of stones can be seen at these sites. Many other kirkyards have examples.

63. Ecclesmachan WL
NT 058 736

64. Humbie EL
NT 460 637

65. Inveresk EL
NT 344 720

66. Pencaitland EL
NT 443 690

67. **Temple ML**
    NT 315 587

68. **Tranent EL**
    NT 402 733

69. **Uphall WL**
    NT 060 722.

CASTLES AND LARGE HOUSES
1100 – 1900 AD

The powerful Anglo-Norman families who appear in Scotland during the reign of David I in the early part of the 12th century built their strongholds in the form of motte-and-bailey castles, with the lord's house on top of a large mound and a courtyard at its base protected by a palisade, in which were built ancillary buildings such as stables, barns, a chapel and workshops. A puzzlingly small number are known in Lothian. The later castle at Yester was built into the side of earlier castle remains. Another one survives at North Berwick without any later buildings on it.

Lothian does however possess some of the finest 13th and 14th-century castles in Scotland, at Tantallon, Dirleton, Hailes and Yester. These testify to the position of Lothian as the corridor of advance from the south for invading armies heading towards Edinburgh and Stirling and the north. All were castles of enclosure, with buildings set inside strong defensive walls, the main fortified keep at the centre.

Internal conflict inspired by rivalries between the noble families in the 14th and 15th centuries saw the development of the tower-house as the lordly residence and many survive today, in varying degrees of repair. Some are incorporated in later grand mansions, others are restored and inhabited as towers and others are simple stumps of masonry. The tower-house was generally designed as a self-contained defensive structure, containing the hall and private quarters of the lord, the kitchens and stores on three floors, linked by spiral stairs. This form was somewhat restricted in its internal arrangements, a problem solved in some cases by the addition of a wing at right angles or by the use of the thickness of the walls for staircases. The towers were often accompanied by the other necessary buildings such as stables, often within a protective wall known as a barmkin. A good example of this arrangement can be seen at Redhouse near Longniddry.

Unique in this period is the royal palace at Linlithgow, built to replace the buildings destroyed in 1424 by fire. The plan is unparalleled in Scotland, with a courtyard, containing an elaborate fountain (*c.*1535), surrounded by ranges of buildings around the outer walls with a stair tower at each corner. The plan seems to be based on the plans of late 14th-century fortified manors of north-east England, but construction of the buildings seems to have been an almost continuous process for more than a century. The aim was obviously to create a residence suitable for the monarch within a defensive structure.

The 16th century saw the increased use of artillery and limited alterations were made to castles and tower-houses to take account of this, with some addition of gun loops and the construction of specific artillery fortifications, such as the blockhouse built to protect Dunbar harbour and castle between 1515 and 1523. Dunbar was the base of the Duke of Albany, regent of Scotland after the death of James IV at Flodden and the blockhouse was to allow the firing of cannon at English invaders. Elsewhere, Tantallon was reinforced in the first half of the 16th century with gun loops in the east tower and main walls. An artillery fortification was built outside the bailey.

The military campaigns of the English between 1544 and 1549 saw great damage done to Lothian, with widespread destruction. Notable in the campaigns was the battle of Pinkie on 10 September 1547 when the Scots were routed by the Earl of Somerset on the level ground to the east of Inveresk church. In the later part of the campaigns a series of fortifications were built by both the English and the Scots (with the help of their French allies). The remains of most of these, ramparts of earth surrounded by ditches, have been completely removed. The largest were around Haddington, erected by the English to protect themselves from the siege of the Scots and French in 1548–9. The site at Dunglass, known as the French Fort, was in fact built by the English under Lord Grey, as part of a series of fortifications to control access along the coastal route. The other parts of these fortifications have been destroyed.

From the later part of the 16th century and into the early 17th century more peaceful conditions prevailed and a new type of house developed for the local nobility, the laird's house. Still based on the tower-house form, these new houses were more concerned with appearance and comfort than defensive capabilities. Decorative features, such as turrets, became more apparent, walls were thinner and external stairs were added and generally the L-plan house was the norm. The interiors of the houses were often richly decorated with tapestries and painted ceilings and walls. Around these new mansions were laid out formal gardens and woodland policies were planted, creating a harmonious whole. Within these policies doocots were often built, not only to provide birds for meat but also as decorative architectural features. A remarkable number have survived, from the 16th century onwards. There are two main types, the circular 'beehive' and the rectangular 'lectern'.

Throughout the 17th and the first half of the 18th centuries most of these laird's houses were built in the local tradition of style and materials and of relatively small scale. A certain number showed signs of a grander design, with the growth of symmetry in their architectural arrangements and the appearance of named architects responsible for these schemes. The buildings were part of the new classical tradition, based on the architecture of Greece and Rome, inspired by the Italian architect Palladio. Between 1750 and 1800 Scottish architects, led by the Adam family (father William and his sons) built new houses, designed sumptuous interiors and modified existing mansions under the patronage of the rich. These houses sat at the centre of the 'improved' estates, symbols of the agricultural and mineral wealth of the county. As the houses grew grander, so did the estates that surrounded them. The more formal, intimate gardens of the 17th century were replaced by large parklands, planted in the Romantic style, where large areas of the countryside were remodelled to form lakes and picturesque settings for the classical mansions at their centres.

The 19th century saw another architectural fashion evolve, the Scottish baronial style, where houses of the scale of the neo-classical period were embellished with decorative features derived from the castle architecture such as turrets and stair-towers, with none of the symmetry of the neo-classical movement. Two of the greatest local exponents of this style were William Burn and David Bryce who worked in the first half of the 19th century.

Castles, tower-houses and laird's houses: 1100 – 1800 AD

Within this list, all sites have been included where there is visible evidence for the original structure, although this can be hidden to a greater or lesser degree by later alterations.

1. Abercorn WL
   NT 083 794
The site of the 15th/16th-century tower is covered by a mound of earth, creating a landscape feature in the designed landscape. The walls of the tower were revealed by excavation in 1963 and part of a glazed tile pavement was found.

2. Alderstone WL
   NT 044 663
A 16th-century tower-house at the north end of the building, extended by the addition of a wing in 1626 by Patrick Kinloch.

3. Auldhame EL
   NT 602 846
The ruins of the main block of a late 16th-century laird's house survive in poor condition, with only the east end surviving to three storeys, with two projecting wings. The basement appears to have been the kitchen, with a large fireplace and an oven. A kitchen midden associated with the building has been found to the W.

4. Ballencrieff House EL
   NT 488 783
The shell, destroyed by fire in 1868 but undergoing restoration at the time of writing, of the late 16th/early 17th-century house of John Murray, first Lord Elibank, was a

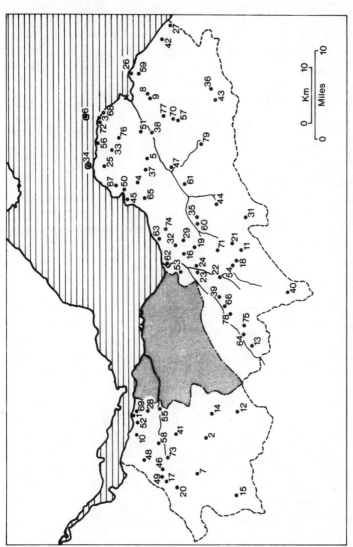

7. Castles

typical L-shaped tower, with vaulted kitchens in the basement of the main block, a hall at first floor and chambers above. This was subsequently extended by the addition of an extension and matching wing to create a U-shaped front. The whole was remodelled by the 5th Lord Elibank in 1730 who rebuilt the original main block and filled the gap between the projecting wings.

5. Barnes Castle EL
NT 529 766

An unusual late 16th-century castle, built by John Seton of Barnes, on an axial plan with large square towers projecting from the corner angles of an enclosure with walls 1m thick, with intermediate towers along the internal walls. It was apparently never completed after the death of Seton in 1594 and survives only to first floor level, with the cellars giving it the local name of 'The Vaults'. The main buildings lay along the E side of the courtyard, forming a large mansion along the whole length of the range, with wings projecting along the side walls.

6. Bass Castle EL
NT 602 873

On the island of the Bass Rock, formed of a volcanic plug, stands the ruin of the castle, believed to have been built in the 16th century. It was dismantled after the siege of 1691–4 when a small group of escaped Jacobite prisoners, supported by the French, held out for three years, although Covenanters were imprisoned here by Charles II in the late 17th century, including John Blackadder, minister of Traquair, whose prison chamber still has the name 'Blackadder's lodging'. The 16th-century curtain wall survives on the only accessible side of the island, on which cannon were mounted, with a range of buildings behind it. A second wall to the east encloses the landing area and has a half-moon battery at the end.

7. Bathgate Castle WL
NS 981 681

South of the railway, adjacent to Guildiehaugh playing fields,

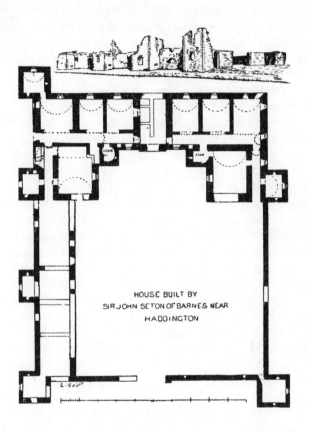

HOUSE BUILT BY
SIR JOHN SETON OF BARNES NEAR
HADDINGTON

Site Plan 6. Barnes Castle. Plan and View (5)

a low mound 2–3m high lies inside two ditches. It was apparently the stronghold of the barony which was part of the dowry of Marjory Bruce who married Walter, High Steward of Scotland. He died in 1328 and the site appears not to have been occupied long after that.

8.   Belton Tower EL
   NT 642 765
A ruined tower-house on the banks of the Biel Burn has a
basement of two barrel-vaulted chambers.

9.   Biel EL
   NT 635 759
The vaulted basement of the house, which was extensively
remodelled in 1760 and the 19th century, is the only
identifiable part of the original structure and consists of
vaulted chambers at the E end of the building.

10. * The Binns WL
   NT 051 786
A three-storey laird's house, originally built in the 1620s by
Thomas Dalyell which was enlarged by his son General Tam
Dalyell, with the addition of a W wing to create one of the
earliest examples in Scotland of a symmetrical design around
a courtyard. The whole was remodelled in the early 19th
century when it was enlarged and the mock castle features of
turrets and battlements were added. Internally much survives
of the decoration of both the original house, particularly the
fine decorated plaster ceilings and General Tam's alterations.
National Trust for Scotland.

11. * Borthwick Castle ML
   NT 369 597
A fine castle, well-preserved, in a picturesque location. Built
by Sir William Borthwick after 1430, it consists of a main
block within a triangular barmkin defensive circuit which has
a round tower of 16th-century date giving cover to the
entrance gate in this corner. The tower is an exceptionally
solid construction, 25m high, with two massive towers on the
W front, either side of the entrance. Internally are three main
floors, all vaulted, linked by stairs built into the walls, which
are 4.3m thick. The main (first) floor contains the kitchen
and a magnificent lord's hall with a pointed vault 9m high,
with service and private chambers situated in the two wings.
The castle was apparently much damaged by Cromwell and

the castle was lost by the Borthwicks in 1672.

12. Bridge Castle WL
NS 943 709

South of Westfield, originally a 16th-century L-shaped tower-house of three storeys, with a secondary wing added in the 17th century. Further additions were made in the late 19th century when the castle was restored.

13. Brunston Castle ML
NT 202 582

The ruins of a 16th-century castle, with a carved date of 1568 and the arms of the Crichton family visible, built on a courtyard plan, with the house on the SE side and a projecting square tower at the N angle, both originally consisting of two main storeys and an attic. The main block, with a stair tower projecting from the facade, had a hall and private chambers over the kitchen and stores. The castle was surrounded by a deep ditch which was recorded in the 19th century. Four low mounds enclosed by a ditch, 100m to the E, are probably a fish pond.

14. Cairns Castle WL
NT 090 605

The vaulted basement and main hall storey of the late 15th-century L-plan tower of the Crichtons are preserved as a ruin, overlooking Harperrig Reservoir.

15. Cakemuir Castle EL
NT 413 591

A four-storey 16th-century tower, apparently built by an advocate called Adam Wauchope, on the evidence of a carved stone carrying his arms which survives in the later rebuilding. The house has a later extension to the W built in 1761.

16. Carberry Tower EL
NT 364 697

A four-storey tower, built in the mid-16th century, probably by Hugh Rigg, had vaulted rooms at second and fourth floor levels. Gargoyles and a decorated cornice are visible at the top of the tower, as is a wrought-iron firebasket at the NW corner. The tower was extended to the S in 1598, with a stair-turret visible, and further extensions were made to this wing in the 18th century. The building was made U-shaped by the addition of an E range by the architect David Bryce in c.1860.

17. Carribber or Rob Gibb's Castle WL
   NS 966 752

Fragmentary remains on the right bank of Carribber Glen, attributed to Rob Gibb, who built a castle in c.1540. Walls of late 16th/early 17th-century date stand up to 3m high around a square courtyard which seems to have had oblong blocks of buildings on the N and S sides.

18. Catclune ML
   NT 351 605

The outline of a 16th-century house of the Sinclair family is visible on a rocky promontory of the east side of the Gore Water.

19. Cousland Castle ML
   NT 3774 6837

The site of very ruinous remains of a 17th-century house and enclosure, with earlier remains also visible in the surrounding area.

20. Couston Castle/North Couston Farm WL
   NS 956 712

Fragmentary remains of a 17th-century tower-house of L-shaped plan, with a vaulted cellar. The house was the property of the Hamilton family.

21. * Crichton Castle ML
   NT 380 611

A courtyard surrounded by buildings, forming a stronghold controlling the route south to Gala Water. The original keep, probably built in the late 14th century by John de Crichton, lies in the E, with most of its W wall now missing. Three further ranges were added to it in the 15th century, forming a courtyard, with the gateway to the S, probably beginning after the attack on the castle by the Douglases in 1445 during their rebellion against James II. The 2nd Lord Crichton was his Chancellor. The castle passed to the Earls of Bothwell in the 16th century and the 5th Earl, Francis Stewart, was responsible for major alterations and additions to the castle of which the most spectacular is the N range, which has a facade of large windows with remarkable decoration of projecting diamond rustication, apparently inspired by Italian palaces (Bothwell returned from Italy in 1581). He also built the large buttressed stone stable which still stands nearby. *Historic Scotland.*

22. Dalhousie Castle ML
   NT 323 637

A large and solid L-shaped tower built in the mid-15th century within a curtain wall. Later additions in the 17th,18th and 19th centuries have filled in the space around the original tower which was built by the Ramsay family and occupied by them until the early 20th century. The Ramsays are known to have had an earlier castle on the site from the 13th century, which was held against Henry IV of England.

23. Dalkeith ML
   NT 333 679

The remains of the 15th-century tower-house of the Morton family are incorporated within the later house. Originally a tower alone within a courtyard, further blocks were added in the courtyard, on the NW where a range with a hall was built and on the NE. These buildings were then built into the early neo-classical mansion built between 1702 and 1711 by James Smith for the Duchess of Monmouth, daughter of the 2nd Earl of Buccleuch. The house was repaired and refaced by John Adam in 1751–3.

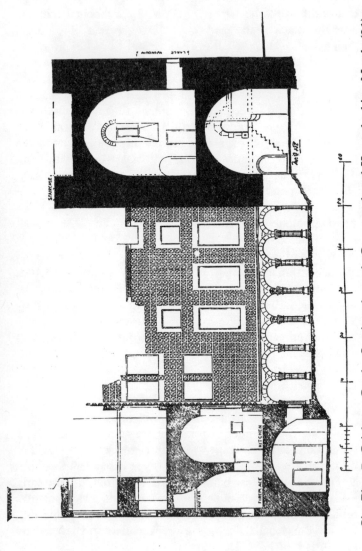

Site Plan 7. Crichton Castle. Section through Courtyard and Keep, looking North (21)

24. Dalkeith Home Farm ML
   NT 348 697

The farmhouse is in fact a 15th-century house, reputedly 'Smeaton Castle'.

25. * Dirleton Castle EL
   NT 515 840

A castle is recorded here in 1225, built by the Anglo-Norman de Vaux family. In its original form it was a curtain wall on much the same line as the existing wall, with circular towers at SE and NE angles. At the SW corner was the main block, still surviving, with a triangular inner court with a main 'drum' tower, with walls 3m thick, which contained the lord's hall. Two other towers project out from the court on the other sides. The castle was captured by the English in 1298 but subsequently regained by the Scots and demolished by them. In the 14th and 15th centuries the Halyburtons, who had gained ownership of the castle by marriage, built the E block along the curtain wall with cellars, bakery, kitchens and chapel. They also built the main entrance and drawbridge. The castle was subsequently altered in the 16th century by the Ruthvens who enclosed the inner court of the original main block with a new building. The castle was bombarded by Cromwell's troops under General Monk in November 1650 and was soon lost. It was left to decay after its purchase by Sir John Nisbet in 1663. He built a new mansion at Archerfield to the N of the village.

26. Dunbar EL
   NT 679 793

The harbour of Dunbar was strategically important, as the best haven north of Berwick and was continually under the threat of attack. The courtyard castle of the Earl of Dunbar is known to have been fought over by the English and Scots in 1297. In 1338 Black Agnes, the Duchess of Dunbar, held out against the English. It was demolished by order of Parliament in 1488, but rebuilt by James IV in the 1490s. After Flodden the Duke of Albany built a blockhouse on the spur south of the castle. Further fortifications were added by the French in the 1550s, but the whole was ordered to be demolished by order of Parliament in 1567 after Mary fled there in 1565. The later harbour works and stormy weather have caused further damage subsequently. The castle was of courtyard type with corner towers, with a forework of the late 15th century, of which the walls survive. Of the apartments little can be seen except the cellars on the SW side. The blockhouse of the Duke of Albany was an irregular octagon with walls 2.5m thick, pierced by gunports to provide artillery cover for the castle and is the best preserved part of the site. A battery on Lamer Island was built as coastal defences in 1781 during the American Wars of Independence.

27. Dunglass EL
NT 763 718
The remains of the earthworks of the 'French Fort', actually built by the English in the late 1540s lie on the high ground on the W side of the burn.

28. * Duntarvie WL
NT 091 765
In process of restoration, Duntarvie is a late 16th-century oblong house with square towers on the N angles, possibly built for James Durham. It was inhabited until the late 19th century.

29. Elphinstone Castle EL
NT 390 698
Partially demolished as a result of subsidence, this 15th-century rectangular tower was originally three storeys with the hall and kitchen on the third floor. The lands had been held by the Elphinstones since the 13th century.

30. Ewes EL
NT 434 448
The site of a tower-house, completely demolished to ground level, within a barmkin wall forming a courtyard around the tower.

31. Fala Luggie EL
NT 425 590

A small keep, probably of early 17th-century date, 8m wide, of which only the SE wall, more than 1m thick, survives. Windows are visible at first floor level, as are the sills of second floor windows.

32. * Falside Castle EL
NT 378 710

Restored in the 1980s, this is a four-storey tower-house of the 15th century with an L-shaped extension built in the 16th century.

33. * Fenton EL
NT 543 821

The three-storey remains of a late 16th-century tower, with walls more than 1m thick which was held by Patrick Whytelaw until 1587 before passing to Sir John Carmichael. Built on an L-shaped plan, the main block contained a hall at first floor level with private chambers above which could be reached by the small staircases visible as turrets at the upper levels.

34. Fidra EL
NT 514 867

Castle Tarbet survives as only a short length of wall on a rocky promontory on the SE corner of the island.

35. Fountainhall EL
NT 427 677

A good example of a small mansion built in the late 16th century as a three-storey house to which extensions were made by John Pringle after he purchased the estate in 1635. The house, formerly known as Woodhead, became the administrative and judicial seat of the barony of Fountainhall after its purchase by John Lauder in 1685, and the jougs attached to the S wall of the house are a physical reminder of this part of the house's history.

36. Gamelshiel EL
NT 649 648

The fragmentary remains of the N wall and vaulted cellar of a tower-house on the N side of Summer Hill next to Whiteadder Reservoir.

37. * Garleton Castle EL
NT 510 768

The badly damaged ruins of what appears to be a late 16th-century structure, built by Sir John Seton of Garleton. Only the E and N walls survive to any height, with a round tower at the SE corner of the E wing. The main range ran at right angles to this wing, with vaults at ground floor level. To the W was a forecourt which had two small houses at the SW (a kitchen) and NW corners.

38. * Hailes Castle EL
NT 575 758

A picturesque ruin of a 13th-century castle of enclosure built by one of the Earls of Dunbar as a tower with a curtain wall to the E, on the banks of the River Tyne. This original block contained a hall over a cellar, with a tower at the W end and a cross wing at the E end. The curtain wall was extended to the W by the Hepburns in the 14th century as far as the tower by the burn which flows into the Tyne at this point and then to the S forming a courtyard with a gate in the S side. The tower was at least three storeys tall having the hall on the third floor, with a cellar and prison below. The rest of the curtain wall is also 14th century. The two towers were linked by a further range of buildings added to the S face of the curtain wall, apparently in the 15th century. It is believed that the first floor level of this range was a chapel. *Historic Scotland.*

39. * Hawthornden ML
NT 286 637

A ruinous 15th-century tower of the Douglas family on a high rock platform overlooking the river valley of the North Esk. The tower is a shell of at least three floors, with a pit prison visible. A screen wall around the courtyard has a 17th-century house restored from the north range of medieval buildings by the poet Sir William Drummond in 1638, on an L-shaped plan, although it has been subsequently altered internally by later occupants.

Below the castle in the cliffs (NT 2862 6367) are a network of caves and passages, traditionally associated with Robert the Bruce, but of uncertain date. One of the caves has a fireplace, windows, seats, cupboards and a well.

40. Hirendean Castle ML
NT 298 512

Only the S wall remains standing of the 16th-century tower of Mark Ker which originally had three storeys.

41. Houston House, Uphall WL
NT 052 713

The house of Sir Thomas Shairp, the King's Advocate, built *c.* 1600, was an L-shaped tower with a vaulted kitchen at ground floor level, with limited alterations of the 18th and 19th centuries and an extension of the 1970s. A range of buildings called the Woman House to the N of an enclosed courtyard is believed to be contemporary with the original house and was vaulted at ground floor level for brewhouse, bakehouse and dairy, with servants' residences above.

42. Innerwick Castle EL
NT 735 737

The Hamilton family castle, of 15th/16th-century date perches on a rocky promontory. Only the lower part of the keep survives on the S side of an enclosure originally surrounded by a stone wall, with a vaulted kitchen at the SE corner with a hall over it. A ditch is visible to the W, on the only side not protected by the natural defences of the burn.

43. Johnscleugh EL
NT 631 644

The two-storey remains of a fortified house at the head of Whiteadder Water, probably a 17th-century remodelling of a

16th-century building.

44. Keith Marischal EL
NT 449 643

Built in 1589 by George Keith, of the Keith family who were Grand Marischals of Scotland, this was a long rectangular house with a vaulted ground floor. The house fell victim to baronialisation in 1889.

45. Kilspindie Castle EL
NT 462 800

North of Aberlady, the stump of a late 16th-century tower built by Patrick Douglas survives to a height of 2m with a doorway and a gunloop visible.

46. Kipps WL
NS 988 739

All that is left of the house built *c.*1625–6 is an oblong block, originally three-storeys high, with two stair towers and vaults containing two separate kitchens.

47. * Lennoxlove EL
NT 515 720

Originally known as Lethington (renamed in 1703) the estate was acquired by the Maitlands in 1385. A massive, three-storey L-plan tower with walls 3m thick was built by the Maitlands in the 15th century. The hall lay at first floor level, occupying the whole floor and was restored and decorated by Robert Lorimer in 1912. It was extended to the E by John Maitland in 1626 when he also enlarged the windows of the tower and provided an easier staircase. A tower was built at the SE end of the extension in 1644. A scheme for a neo-classical remodelling of the house in the 18th century was not carried through and only the range to the NW was built, along with a coach-house. Alterations to the east wing and the 1644 tower were made in the early 19th century.

48. * Linlithgow Palace WL
NT 002 773

Built on the site of the earlier royal manor house and 12th-century parish kirk which were destroyed by fire in 1424, is one of the great buildings of medieval Scotland. The site had been used by Edward I of England as a base for his siege operations at Stirling in 1301–2. Of the buildings now standing, an early 16th-century gatehouse gives access to a courtyard with an elaborate fountain built by James V at its centre. The courtyard is surrounded by ranges of buildings

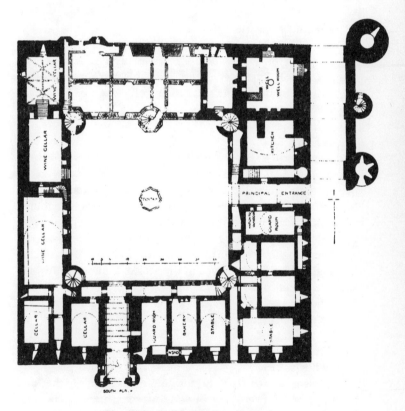

Site Plan 8. Linlithgow Palace.
Plan of Ground Floor (**48**)

with a stair tower at each corner, built from 1425 until the mid-16th century in three main episodes (1425–37, 1490–1513 and 1534–41). There is still considerable dispute as to the order and date of construction of the various elements of the palace and it is difficult to link the known periods of work with specific building remains. The functional arrangements of the ranges in its later occupation in the late 16th and early 17th centuries are known. The S wing held the chapel, and the 'Hall', the W range was the site of the 'Great Hall' and the 'Presence Chamber' and the E wing contained the kitchen and the royal apartments. The N range, rebuilt in 1618–20, had a large number of chambers. *Historic Scotland.*

49. Lochcote Castle WL
   NT 977 730

The remains of a 17th-century castle survive as a vaulted chamber, 4.5m high, which are probably the remains of an angle tower, with a window in each wall.

50. * Luffness EL
   NT 475 804

A three-storey tower-house, on a T-shaped plan, with the stair in the short arm, its construction has been dated to the late 16th century by a panel over the door dated 1584, although the estate was in the ownership of the Hepburns from the middle of the 15th century and the buildings may in fact belong to this period or earlier. The original building was extended in several episodes in the 19th century, being baronialised by David Bryce in the 1840s. Square earthworks and deep ditches around the building may be a French fort of 1549 built to cut off the supply lines of the English forces garrisoned at Haddington.

51. Markle EL
   NT 579 775

The walls of the castle stand inside ramparts and ditches and seem to be of two main periods of construction, the first being a rectangular building with walls 1m thick, associated with fragmentary remains of a curtain wall. A later range, whose N wall stands to third floor height, was built on the NE corner of the original building and a small courtyard was enclosed to the N by a wall.

52. Midhope WL
   NT 073 787
A late 16th-century tower of five storeys built by Alexander Drummond which was extended to the E *c.* 1600, an extension which was subsequently enlarged in 1680 by the Earl of Linlithgow.

53. * Monkton House EL
   NT 334 703
A 16th-century tower of the Hay family of Yester, a small rectangular structure with a vaulted cellar. This was extended in the 17th century by the addition of ranges on the SW and NW (of which only part of the latter survives) forming an L-shaped house and courtyard. The house was remodelled in the mid-18th century by the Falconers after the forfeiture of the estate by the Jacobite Hays.

54. Newbyres Castle ML
   NT 344 615
Only the NE corner of a mid-16th-century L-shaped tower is standing, most of the rest having collapsed in 1881.

55. * Niddry Castle WL
   NT 095 744
A restored late 15th/early 16th-century tower, within its barmkin wall, also known as Niddry-Seton. Built by George, the 4th Lord Seton, the tower is four storeys high, on an L-shaped plan. The hall occupies the whole of the first floor of the main block, with the kitchen in the wing. Cellars lie below the hall and private chambers above, all linked by a spiral stair built inside the wall at the angle between the main block and the wing. Remains of rig and furrow cultivation and field banks are visible in fields around the castle, contemporary with the occupation of the castle.

56. North Berwick EL
NT 561 852

A mound 12m high on the summit of Castle Hill, East Links, with the remains of an earth and stone bank enclosing an area of 32m by 36m. A ditch cuts across the neck of land on the S of the site. This is probably a Norman motte-and-bailey castle.

57. Nunraw EL
NT 597 706

Hidden within later alterations are the remains of a Z-plan tower built by the Hepburns after they acquired the site after the Reformation, consisting of a central rectangular block with square towers on the opposing NE and SW corners. The house was refaced and altered in the 1860s and only the NE tower remains relatively intact in its original form with gargoyles draining the wall-walk.

58. Ochiltree Castle
NT 033 748

A late 16th/early 17th-century laird's house of three storeys on an L-plan, remodelled in the late 17th century by the addition of a kitchen to the wing.

59. Old Lochend House EL
NT 678 780

The ruin of a 17th-century mansion near Dunbar.

60. Ormiston EL
NT 413 677

A two-storey building standing E of the church is the earlier Ormiston House, built in the early 17th century, with a main block and wing and cellars at ground floor level. The later Hall was built in 1745–8 for John Cockburn of Ormiston, extended in 1772 by the Earl of Hopetoun and again in the early 19th century. It is now a ruin.

61. Pilmuir EL
NT 486 694
A small T-shaped house of 1624, orange harled, with two storeys and an attic. The arm of the T is formed by the stair tower which has a further storey at the top. The house was built by William Cairns and his wife Agnes Broun.

62. Pinkie House EL
NT 350 727
Within the buildings of Loretto School is a 16th-century tower built by the Abbot of Dunfermline Abbey, which was acquired by Alexander Seton in 1597. As Earl of Dunfermline he extended and embellished the house after 1613, marking the work with his initials and those of his wife, Lady Hay of Yester, to whose family the house passed in 1694. He added decorative turrets and a parapet to the tower itself, raised the height of the existing wing and built a new wing to the S, with a further wing off this which was never completed beyond second floor level. Internally much of the interior decoration, particularly the plasterwork and painted ceilings of Seton's house, survives.

63. Preston Tower EL
NT 390 741
The shell of a 15th-century tower on an L-plan, enlarged to six storeys in the 17th century and surrounded by a 17th-century enclosure wall. Built by the Hamiltons of Preston, the hall was located on the third floor. The house was burned by the Earl of Hertford in 1544, Cromwell's troops in 1650 and accidentally in 1663, after which the family abandoned it and moved to Preston House.

64. Ravensneuk Castle ML
NT 223 590
A ruinous N wall and gable return are all that are left of the building which was robbed by Sir John Clerk to build a park wall.

65. * Redhouse EL
NT 463 771

A well-preserved ruin, built in two separate episodes, originally by John Laing, Keeper of the Royal Signet in the years around 1600. The earliest phase included a four-storey oblong tower on the north of a courtyard which had a range of rooms on the E side, including a lectern doocot. The tower was subsequently extended to the N, raised in height at the NE corner to 6 storeys and given a wing at its NE corner. The house became derelict after 1746 when the Jacobite sympathies of Sir Alexander Hamilton led to its forfeiture.

66. * Roslin ML
NT 275 628

The picturesque ruin of the 15th-century castle of the Sinclairs, above the North Esk is reached by a stone bridge of 15th/16th-century date, over a man-made defensive gap in the ridge and then through the gatehouse. The keep lay at the SW end of the massive defensive wall along the W side of the enclosure; only the W wall and part of the S return survive. The walls of the keep are almost 3m thick. The wall between the keep and the gatehouse has external triangular buttresses with openings between. The buildings of the E range, a 16th/17th-century house, are restored and inhabited. The hall and kitchen of this rectangular range lie on ground floor level, with three floors of vaulted cellars below, built against the face of the crag. A tower stands at the corner of the range.

67. Saltcoats EL
NT 486 818

A ruin near Dirleton, probably built by Patrick Levingtoun in 1592 (on the evidence of a stone built into a cottage nearby), the castle was inhabited until 1790. It has an unusual and striking W front surviving to five storeys, consisting of two square towers rising from round bases, joined by a large, tall segmented arch pierced by a grand window in the centre. Of the rest, only the S wall of the range behind the entrance survives to any height, with large windows at first floor level presumably lighting the hall. A courtyard surrounded by a screen wall lay to the N, with a vaulted kitchen in the NE angle showing the presence of a second range along the N wall. The doocot to the N probably belonged to the castle.

68. Seacliff Tower EL
NT 612 844

A ruin on exposed cliffs over the Car Rocks, *c.* 650m E of the estate buildings, is a late 16th-century L-plan house. Nearby is the shell of the house built for George Sligo in 1841 which was destroyed by fire in the 20th century.

69. Staneyhill ML
NT 092 785

The ruin of a 17th-century L-plan mansion, with only a hexagonal stair tower and the walls and vaults of the ground floor surviving. The kitchen was at this level with the hall above.

70. Stoneypath Tower EL
NT 595 713

The ruin of a 15th-century tower of the Lyell family, built on an L-plan; the hall occupied the S range. A carved head survives at the end of the E side. The building used to have a conical stone roof.

71. Southside ML
NT 369 639

An L-plan house of the 17th century, remodelled in the mid-19th century.

72. * Tantallon EL
NT 599 850

The earliest reference to this well-preserved and spectacularly-sited castle is in 1374. Built by the Earls of Douglas, the castle was protected a single massive curtain wall, 15m high with a large E tower, cutting off the promontory and a ditch immediately outside. A further ditch forms an enclosure outside the castle, protected by a ravelin on the SW landward side. The curtain wall has three towers,

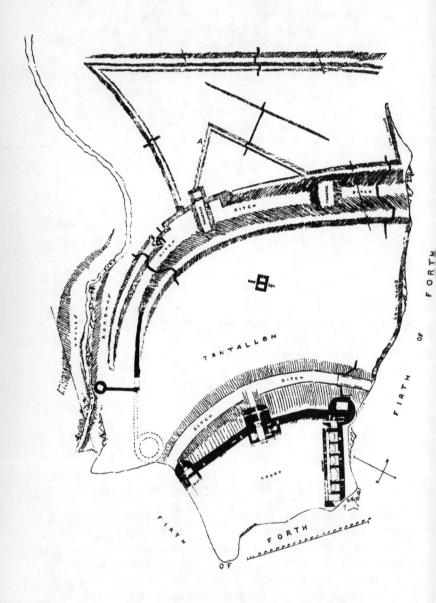

Site Plan 9. Tantallon Castle. Plan of site (**72**)

with a circular tower at the W, known as the Douglas tower, which has a pit prison in its basement and a D-shaped tower at the other end. The main entrance was through the central tower which was much altered and enlarged after the castle was captured by James V in 1529 after a siege. The range of apartments lay on the NW side above the cliffs, with a hall over a vaulted basement. This range was extended to the E in the 16th century with the addition of new rooms, including a kitchen and bakehouse at ground floor level. The sea-gate lay on the E side with a small landing stage. The castle passed back to the Douglas' estates before the English invasion of 1544 and was held until the towers and defences were badly damaged by cannon fired by General Monk over 12 days during the English Civil War of 1650. The castle was allowed to decay from the late 17th century onwards. A small landing stage and sea-gate survive NW of the castle. *Historic Scotland.*

73. Tartraven WL
   NT 011 729

At South Mains is the possible site of a homestead 100m by 65m, surrounded by a five-sided moat, with a ditch 11m wide by 0.8m deep which has been destroyed on the N side. This may be the earliest site of Tartraven Castle whose site is now lost.

74. Tranent EL
   NT 405 730

The ruin of the late 16th-century tower, three storeys high, lies close to the parish church. The tower is vaulted at ground floor level; each floor has two rooms.

75. Uttershill Castle ML
   NT 239 594

The ruin of a late 16th-century mansion of the Prestons of Craigmillar, built on an oblong plan, stands to two-thirds height. Inside, the W side has a vaulted cellar at ground level with a hall above it, and the E side was a kitchen with a private chamber over. A straight stair, now collapsed, ran between them.

76. Waughton Castle EL
NT 567 809

To the SE of Old Waughton are the remains of the castle; only a small projecting wing survives, probably of 16th-century date. The castle is mentioned in 1395.

77. Whittingehame Castle EL
NT 602 732

A three-storey L-shaped house from the late 15th or early 16th century, on a site acquired by the Douglas family in the 14th century. The castle's 17th-century outbuildings lie on the W. A possible gun platform is visible as a mound to the SE.

78. Woodhouselee ML
NT 257 616

Three vaults on the top of a high rock are the remains of the castle, built in the 16th or early 17th century by the Sinclairs. Limited excavation of a small building in the centre of the ruin showed it to be possibly a kitchen.

79. * Yester Castle EL
NT 556 667

The castle is situated on a peninsula with precipitous natural defences on two sides and is protected on the S by a ditch 30m wide and 6m deep. A second ditch lies at the N end. A curtain wall runs around the interior; the buildings inside these have mostly been levelled, but some survive to considerable height. On the E side of the curtain wall was a three-storey range, dating to the 14th century. On the W another range leads to the Goblin Ha', an oblong chamber built of massive masonry blocks, which is probably the undercroft of a 13th-century tower which was later reduced in height. This tower had seemingly been dug into the side of a pre-existing motte mound. A bridge pier survives in the centre of Hopes Water and masonry survives which suggests a bridge to the S as well.

Country houses: 1700 – 1900 AD

These represent the best examples of their type, where not encumbered by later accretions. For further details of their architecture, refer to the excellent Lothian volume of the *Buildings of Scotland* series. These houses are all worth seeing; remember that all are privately owned. As most lie at the centre of large estates, four-figure grid references are given.

1. Archerfield EL
   NT 50 80
This derelict shell of a house was originally built in the late 17th century on three sides of a courtyard and was redesigned by Robert Adam in 1790 on a T-plan.

2. Arniston ML
   NT 30 60
Built by William Adam in 1726 for Robert Dundas with a grand nine-bay frontage. The formal gardens contemporary with the house were obscured by the parkland redesigned by Thomas White in 1791. The walled garden contains architectural fragments from the front of the mid-17th-century Old Parliament House in Edinburgh.

3. Auchendinny House ML
   NT 25 61
A Palladian villa on the small scale, built by Sir William Bruce for John Inglis of Lanarkshire and completed by 1707.

4. Bonnytoun House WL
   NT 00 70
A neo-Tudor exterior with a Grecian interior, built *c.* 1840.

5. Lauderdale House, Dunbar EL
   NT 68 79
A fine house, built 1790–2 by R and J Adam, which has been damaged by later alterations, particularly by the later military occupants when it was used as a barracks.

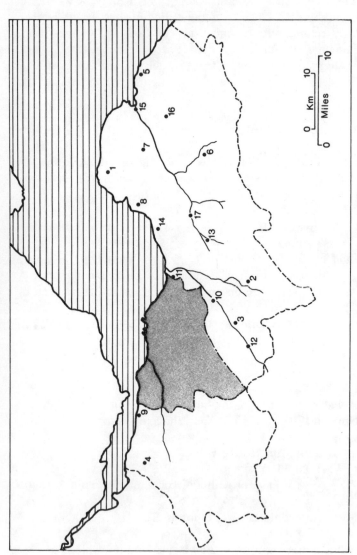

8. Country Houses 1700 – 1900

6.   Yester House, Gifford EL
   NT 53 68

A severe box-shaped house of 1699–1728 by James Smith
and Alexander MacGill for the Hay family, with the interior
much improved by William and Robert Adam.

7.   Gilmerton House EL
   NT 50 70

A three-storey house built for the great improving landowner
David Kinloch of Gilmerton in the 1750s.

8.   Gosford House EL
   NT 40 70

A large neo-classical house of the Earl of Wemyss, built
1790–1800 by Robert Adam, extended and altered in the late
19th century.

9.   Hopetoun House WL
   NT 09 79

A vast palace incorporating the house of 1699–1701 on the
W side. The E front was built by William Adam between
1721 and 1748 and the rest was completed by John and his
other sons.

10. Mavisbank ML
   NT 20 60

Sad shell of a beautiful house built by Sir John Clerk and
William Adam.

11. Newhailes EL
   NT 30 70

The centre block was built by James Smith in 1686, altered
by William Adam and the wings finally added before 1757.

12. Penicuik House ML
   NT 25 60

The grounds were laid out by Sir John Clerk in the early 18th
century. His son built the new house in this romantic
landscape from 1761 to his own design. It is considered a

perfect match of Palladian house and romantic designed landscape.

13. Preston Hall ML
   NT 30 60
A large neo-classical house built by Robert Mitchell in 1791.

14. Seton House EL
   NT 40 70
Seton Palace, a tall L-plan tower, was demolished prior to the construction of the late 18th-century Seton House but the 17th-century garden walls with round corner towers survive. The later house is a fine example of the castle-style house, built by Robert Adam in 1789.

15. Tyninghame EL
   NT 60 80
A 17th-century house surrounded by later additions (by William Burn 1828) on land which has been occupied since 1094. In the 16th century the Lauders of the Bass lived on the Bass Rock in summer and here during the winter.

16. Whittingehame EL
   NT 60 70
A grand example of Grecian architecture by Sir Robert Smirke for James Balfour in 1817.

17. Winton House EL
   NT 42 70
A 16th-century house, burned by the Earl of Hertford in 1547, later restored and then embellished in 1620–7 by the second Earl of Winton using the King's master mason to produce a fine Scottish Renaissance house.

INDUSTRY AND COMMUNICATIONS
1600 – 1900 AD

For much of prehistory and indeed much of the historical period, industry was small-scale, often carried out by individual craftspeople. From the medieval period onwards, there is a growth in the scale and diversity of the industries carried out and a parallel expansion in the exploitation of natural resources to supply those industries. Medieval pottery kilns are known from Colstoun in East Lothian, which were active in the 12th to 15th centuries, producing cooking pots and jugs which are found all over Lothian. Kilns producing exotic decorated glazed floor tiles have been found close to North Berwick priory.

Most of the industries which flourished between the 18th century and the earlier years of this century have now disappeared, leaving remarkably few traces. The real legacy of this industrialisation has been a fundamental change in the settlement and employment pattern of Lothian. Industry, and the changes in farming practice after the 18th-century Improvement measures, brought a dispersed rural population together in the towns.

Coal was the richest mineral resource of Lothian. The Midlothian coalfield, laid down some 400 million years ago, lies south and east of Edinburgh. Smaller fields lie in East Lothian and at the extreme western boundary of West Lothian. Close to the coast the coal is easily accessible from ground level and was first mined under the control the monks of Newbattle Abbey at Aldhamer (later Prestonpans) in 1209. They later exploited the coal around Newbattle itself. In the 19th century Lothian Coal Company was run by the Marquis of Lothian, a descendant of the last Abbot of Newbattle. Evidence of medieval mining elsewhere survives at Birsley Brae near Tranent, where the coal was extracted by the digging of individual round shafts which were expanded at their base, from which they derive their name of bell-pits. From the 17th century, deeper seams were exploited by sinking deep shafts and working long tunnels through the broad coal seams. The 18th and 19th centuries saw a massive expansion in mining, led by entrepreneurs such as the Earl of Winton. Since the maximum production period of the 1920s and 1930s, decline has been gradual; only one working deep pit is now in operation at Monktonhall. The future is seen in massive open-cast sites such as the one at Bindwells near Tranent.

The mining of coal created a demand for workers; new settlements grew up near the pits from early times, although miners in the 17th and 18th centuries were treated as no better than serfs, with few legal rights. Women and children were employed in large numbers. The 19th-century expansion of mining saw improvements in conditions above and below ground. Entirely new villages were built by the mineowners for the workers, such as Newtongrange and Rosewell in Midlothian. The latter is still a fine example of the type, with well-preserved single-storey brick cottages.

Oil shale, which occurs in West Lothian, was the other major fuel industry of the area from the 19th century. The process of extracting oil from the shale beds was discovered by John 'Paraffin Young' in the middle part of the century and he opened his first mine at Bathgate in 1850. By 1871 there were 51 works in production. By-products from the process allowed other industries to grow, such as caustic soda, wax, brickmaking (from the shale), detergent and ammonium sulphate for fertilisers. Competition from crude oil saw the end of the industry and today the only remains are the vast bings of West Lothian, formed from the waste shale after the removal of the oil.

It was the easy availability and abundance of coal, however, which attracted a variety of industries to Lothian. The presence of clays suitable for firing along the coastal plain of East Lothian saw the development of potteries, brickworks and tileworks in the area from Portobello to Prestonpans. In East Lothian the most famous pottery was the Cadell works, founded in 1751 by William Cadell. They produced a hard form of pottery called stoneware, glazed using the local salt and a fine tableware known as creamware, made from imported clay and ground up flints, which were brought in through Morrison's Haven. Pottery-making expanded and spread along the coast in the following century. Other factories produced the distinctive red pantiles which are typical of East Lothian. Bricks were made, but not used extensively in Lothian, with the exception of the chimneys of steadings and in the construction of the mining villages. A large quantity of bricks were exported.

Coal from East Lothian was used in the production of salt, the major preservative for food before refrigeration. It was extracted from seawater, by evaporation in large heated pans made of iron, from Cockenzie to Prestongrange. Again it was the monks of Newbattle Abbey who were the first producers, after they were granted possession of the harbour of Aldhamer, a place whose name changed as a result of the salt industry, first to Saltpreston and then to Prestonpans. The industry expanded greatly in the 17th century and was highly profitable. As in the coal industry, saltworkers had few rights. Competition from elsewhere saw the decline of the industry; the last pan ceased production in 1959.

The fine barley of East Lothian and ready supplies of water made brewing an important industry in Lothian; the brewery which still produces beer at Belhaven was founded in the 13th century by monks from the priory on the Isle of May. Most towns had their own breweries from the 17th century onwards, now lost to the predations of the larger companies. Whisky distilling was also carried out at the Magdalene Distillery in Linlithgow and the still-functioning Glenkinchie Distillery near Pencaitland.

The easily available stone resources of Lothian, such as the sandstones which give the buildings of East Lothian their characteristic appearance, the hard volcanic whinstones, used in rubble walling and as roadstone; and limestones used for the production of lime and cement, have been quarried for many years. Small quarries for building stone can be found all over the three counties. The discovery of the benefits of spreading lime on acid soils in the 17th century saw the growth of a new industry. Limestone is burned slowly with coal to produce lime, a process originally carried out using clamp kilns, simple horseshoe-shaped structures of stone and turf. Lime was later produced in greater quantities in large stone-built kilns, constantly fed from the top with coal and limestone. Many of these monumental structures survive well. In the east, around Dunbar, where limestone is plentiful but coal does not occur in great quantities, a harbour was built at Skateraw specifically for the delivery of coal along the coast.

A range of other industries were practised on a smaller scale, including soapmaking at Prestonpans, gunpowder manufacture at Roslin Glen and papermaking in the Penicuik area, using water power. Textiles were always a minor industry, despite attempts in the 18th century to encourage their production. Weaving of wool was carried out in Haddington in particular and in other villages such as Athelstaneford and Aberlady.

For many centuries, communication and transport across Lothian and beyond was difficult. Most roads were simple tracks with no surfacing; the only substantial structures were fine stone bridges built at river crossings. These were obviously a source of civic pride, as the surviving examples at Haddington (Abbey Bridge), Musselburgh (Old Roman Bridge) and East Linton show. The increasing industrialisation and prosperity commerce brought demanded improvements. The introduction of turnpike roads in the 18th century, where upkeep was funded by the levying of tolls, saw a dramatic improvement in the quality of the roads. New links to Glasgow and the west were made by the Edinburgh and Glasgow Union Canal, built between 1818 and 1822. This survives as a striking achievement today, carried on high aqueducts across the Almond and Avon valleys.

One of the earliest railways in the world was built in East Lothian to link Tranent with Cockenzie in 1722, carrying coal from the mines to the harbour. It was a waggonway embankment, with wooden rails on top. The natural incline took the waggons down to Cockenzie; horses pulled them back uphill. A stretch of this waggonway still survives. A later example, built at Pinkie in 1767, was the first to use wrought iron rails. In 1842 the main Edinburgh to Glasgow railway was opened, a revolution in transportation and opportunities for trade. By 1850 the main line from Edinburgh to Berwick had been built by the North British Railway Company. The route to Carstairs and the west coast line was opened in the same year by the Caledonian Railway. Branch lines followed, mainly to service the coalfields and growing industrial centres. Others, such as the branch to Haddington and the singularly unsuccessful line to Gifford, were for agricultural produce. Passenger transport was a by-product of the expansion of the railways and the branch lines to North Berwick and the coast of East Lothian helped create holiday resorts. The railways also enabled the phenomenon of commuting from the smaller towns of Lothian into Edinburgh to work.

The sea was always important, both for fishing and also for communication and trade, particularly before the advent of the railways. Leith was one of the major ports of Europe. Smaller harbours existed all along the coast, particularly in East Lothian and were often developed by local entrepreneurs to assist with the exploitation of their landholdings. Many of these are now abandoned or greatly reduced in the scale of their use.

Industrial Sites

Although much physical evidence for this period has already disappeared, a considerable amount still exists, much of it unrecorded in any systematic fashion. The following sites have been selected to give as wide a view as possible of the range of industrial remains in Lothian.

Mining

1. **Tranent EL**
    NT 393 729

At Birsley Brae, W of Tranent, the depressions of infilled bell-pits are visible in woodland, representing the traces of medieval coal-mining. Other sites are visible in the fields between Ormiston and Tranent. The construction of the A1 dual carriageway at Bankton, N of Tranent, revealed an area of bell-pits.

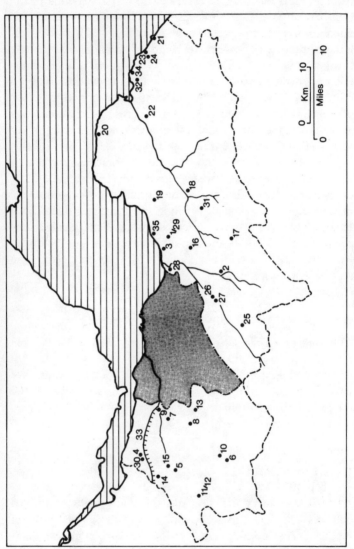

9. Industrial Sites

2. Newtongrange ML
NT 333 636

Lady Victoria Colliery. Sunk in 1890–4 by the Lothian Coal Company, the extensive buildings and surviving machinery are open as a museum and visitor centre. The village contains seven rows of single-storey brick cottages built for the miners.

3. Prestongrange EL
NT 373 737

The sole surviving beam pumping engine in Scotland, built in 1874 to drain the 238m deep shaft. The site has been preserved as a museum complex, with the engine house, colliery power station and a 24 chamber Hoffman brick kiln the only survivors of the extensive industries which once flourished at the site. Nearby stood potteries, chemical works, saltworks and a flint mill, all served by the now lost Morrison's Haven which was built soon after 1526 by the monks of Newbattle Abbey.

4. Bonnytoun Hill WL
NT 015 781

Traces of old coalworkings are visible in the face of the hill. Some date back to the reign of James III; the mines were last used in the General Strike of 1926.

Remains of many other collieries can be seen around the countryside in East, West and Midlothian and many are marked on Ordnance Survey maps. Extreme care must be taken if exploring any of them, as old mines can be dangerous.

5. Silvermine WL
NS 989 716

Three depressions in a field S of Cairnpapple Hill are all that remain of a silver mine opened in 1606 and taken over by James VI in 1608. By May 1608 there were 59 employees in a single shaft; at least 7 shafts are known. Let to a private firm in 1613, the mine closed in 1614.

Oil-shale workings

No substantial remains of refineries or retorts of the industry survive, but substantial bings dominate the eastern part of West Lothian.

6. **Addiewell WL NT 005 628**
7. **Broxburn WL NT 08 73**
8. **Pumpherston WL NT 07 69**
9. **Winchburgh WL NT 097 747**
10. **West Calder WL NT 010 640**

Brickworks

11. **Bathgate WL**
    NS 944 680
The late 19th-century Hoffman kilns and their tall chimneys survive from the Atlas and Etna Brickworks.

Limekilns

12. **Bathgate ML**
    NS 978 702
Ballencrieff limekilns, a group of three kilns.

13. **Kirknewton ML**
    NT 095 683
A group of late 18th-century kilns, including an unusual four-draw kiln with a semicircular tunnel giving access to the rear draw-hole. A second group of three kilns lies to the S.

14. **Torphichen WL**
    NS 977 747
A range of three kilns, with three clamp kilns nearby.

15. **Wairdlaw WL**
    NS 996 730
An early 19th-century pair of kilns with the undisturbed remains of the quarry and a mine to the N.

16. Cranston ML
1. NT 376 689
2. NT 411 625

1. Cousland Lime Works. Ruins of three kilns can be seen at NT 375 686. The quarry has been in existence since the 16th century.
2. Magazine Wood. Limekilns and quarries are visible.

17. Crichton ML
NT 392 616

An early 19th-century pair of kilns, at right angles to each other, with a range of offices and houses nearby.

18. Saltoun EL
NT 473 692

At Middlemains, a pair of 4-draw kilns, which were rebuilt between 1817 and 1820.

19. Gladsmuir EL
NT 457 754

East of the village are the remains of two kilns.

20. North Berwick EL
NT 572 850

A substantial kiln survives at Rhodes.

21. Skateraw EL
NT 737 754

A kiln can be seen by the shore. The small harbour nearby (NT 739 754) was built to allow coal delivery by sea.

22. East Linton EL
NT 602 768

Phantassie. Well-preserved kiln.

23. Dunbar EL
NT 715 774

Catcraig. One double kiln and a range of three others have been restored.

24. Dunbar EL
NT 703 763

Oxwell Mains. The remains of the masonry housing of a wind-driven pump on the edge of a limestone quarry, close to the A1.

Paper mills

25. Penicuik ML
NT 238 598

Valleyfield Paper Mills, founded 1708, still survive as a large group of buildings

26. Lasswade ML
NT 291 650

Founded in 1750, a complex of brick and rubble-built buildings can still be seen.

27. Polton WL
NT 287 647

Founded in 1742, a large complex of buildings are still extant.

Weaving

28. Musselburgh EL
NT 339 723

Esk Net Mills, built from 1867 onwards, are a remarkable collection of buildings, including a spinning mill and all the ancillary buildings.

Railways

Little recording of the surviving structures of the old branch railway system has been done. The lines of many are shown on the Ordnance Survey maps of the area and make fine walks with the chance to do a little industrial archaeology and observation of one's own. Features of all are stations, sidings, bridges and level crossings. The line from Longniddry to

Haddington is maintained as a formal walkway.

29. Tranent EL
NT 398 757 to 403 734

Cockenzie waggonway, opened in 1722 by the York Buildings Co. The track of the first railway in Scotland runs alongside the B6371 and as a path between two hedges.

Brewing

30. Linlithgow WL
NT 008 777

St Magdalene Distillery. Late 18th century in construction, the buildings are currently derelict.

31. Pencaitland EL
NT 443 668

Glenkinchie distillery was founded in c.1840; a group of brick buildings, including a bond store are all that remains of the old distillery within the modern complex.

32. Belhaven EL
NT 665 784

The current brewery was founded in 1709, on a site first used for brewing in the 13th century by monks from the Isle of May in the Forth. Most of the buildings are rebuilt following serious fires in the 19th century, but the cellars and wells of the medieval brewery survive.

Canals

33. The Edinburgh and Glasgow Union Canal WL
Built 1881–82, this canal runs through West Lothian (NT 105 706 to NS 967 778). Numerous bridges and fine aqueducts are visible crossing over the Almond and Avon. Of other ancillary remains, a maintenance depot is still extant at Powflats (WL NT 083 712) and canal stables at Woodcockdale (WL NT 975 759).

Harbours

34. Dunbar EL
NT 679 793

Dunbar's original harbour was at Belhaven to the W. The current harbour works are dated to 1710–30 when a basin was made by excavation of 2.4m of rock and the creation of a curved pier and also to 1844 when the Victoria harbour was built. There are 18th and 19th-century warehouses, granaries and maltings which surround the harbour.

35. Cockenzie EL
NT 398 756

The harbour was built by the Earl of Winton in the 1630s to export coal and salt. It was refurbished in 1722 when the waggonway was built from Tranent. The harbour was completely rebuilt by 1833 by John Cadell to a design by Robert Stephenson.

BIBLIOGRAPHY AND FURTHER READING

The Historic Scotland Series published in association with Batsford offer a good introduction to specific periods and subjects and each includes a bibliography for further reading. Volumes relevant to Lothian include:

Ashmore, P J, (1996) *Neolithic and Bronze Age Scotland*
Breeze, D, (1996) *Roman Scotland: Frontier Country*
Fawcett, R, (1994) *Scottish Abbeys and Priories*
Foster, S M, (1996) *Picts, Gaels and Scots*
Tabraham, C and Grove, D, (1995) *Fortress Scotland and the Jacobites*
Wickham-Jones, C R, (1994) *Scotland's First Settlers*
Yeoman, P, (1995) *Medieval Scotland: an archaeological perspective.*

Other useful books include:
Baldwin, J, (1997) *Exploring Scotland's Heritage: Edinburgh, Lothian and the Borders.* HMSO, Edinburgh
Cruden, S, (1986) *Scottish Medieval Churches.* Donald, Edinburgh
Hanson, W C and Maxwell, G S, (1993) *Rome's North-West Frontier: the Antonine Wall.* Edinburgh University Press, Edinburgh
Hume, J, (1996) *The Industrial Archaeology of Scotland:1 The Lowlands and Borders.* Batsford, London
McWilliam, C, (1978) *The Buildings of Scotland: Lothian.* Penguin, Harmondsworth
Ritchie, G and A, (1981) *Scotland: Archaeology and Early History.* Thames and Hudson, London
Willsher, B, (1985) *Understanding Scottish Graveyards – an interpretive approach.* Chambers, Edinburgh.

Many archaeological objects from Lothian are in the care of the National Museums of Scotland. The new Museum of Scotland, under construction at the time of writing, is due to open in November 1998 and will feature a considerable number of these objects in its displays.

Please check opening times with the Local Tourist Information Centres, Local Authorities or the Scottish Museum Council before visiting any of the following facilities. Some charge for entry.

Scottish Agricultural Museum, Royal Highland Showground, Ingliston.

Prestongrange Industrial Heritage Museum, Prestonpans.

North Berwick Museum, School Road, North Berwick.

Dunbar Under Ground, Townhouse, High Street, Dunbar.

Preston Mill and Phantassie Doocot, near East Linton.

Scottish Mining Museum, Lady Victoria Colliery, Newtongrange.

Almond Valley Heritage Centre, Millfield, Kirkton, Livingston.